TRUST
REPAIR

Praise for *Trust Repair: It IS Possible!*

"Repairing trust in groups is a field many talk about, but few can provide substantive strategies on how to do it. Dr. Wendy Fraser has created a sound model, supported by research and practice, and provides practical tools to use immediately with groups. This book will quickly become an essential handbook for leaders and practitioners."
—Dr. Solomon Uwadaile, President, Trafton-International Consulting Group

"Readers will be drawn to Dr. Fraser's Trust Repair through her relatable stories and simply-stated text. Her extensive research and experience shine through in an understandable process for repairing trust not only in the workplace, but also in personal relationships. Teams will find the many tools and exercises pragmatic for working through their trust issues."
—Mary Beth Colón, Senior Business Systems Analyst (Ret), Bank of New York Mellon

"Trust Repair resonated deeply with both personal trust relationships and my career as a Special Forces Green Beret, where internal team dynamics are vastly complex making it highly valuable to use this model to repair, maintain, and prevent loss of trust for peak efficiency in life and death situations."
—Matthew Savolskis SFC (ret.), MBA, LSSBB

"In both personal and professional applications, Dr. Wendy Fraser's Trust Repair methodology and tools are easily digestible for positive outcomes. Whether you are a c-suite executive, employee, board member, or spouse, it is crucial that you master foundational trust in all these varied relationships. However, we are all human and at some point, repair will have to be done - usually, many times along the way. When this type of reset needs to happen, Trust Repair, is your step by step principle resource."
—Daya V. Fields, Senior Vice President of Marketing and Product Development, Alaffia

"*Dr. Wendy Fraser emphasizes that trust is a critical element to build well-functioning teams at all levels. This book outlines strategies for identifying issues that get in the way and tools for repairing trust within groups. These concepts will help new supervisors lead better, support leaders moving forward when their groups have trust and performance issues, and will be a resource to line staff who lead team projects within the organization.*"
—Kathleen L. Beaumont, Program Development Manager, University of Washington-Tacoma Professional Development Center

"*Wendy's insights in Trust Repair helped me to understand how I had made peace with an abusive father and helped me to forge a functioning relationship with an unfaithful ex-wife for the benefit of our children. I have been lucky enough to train with Wendy personally, and her expertise in human systems is only surpassed by her passion for them. Trust Repair is sure to become a go-to reference for those looking to heal the deep wounds of broken promises.*"
—Name withheld for privacy purposes

"*In this book Wendy clearly explains what it takes to repair trust that has been broken between individuals at work. After helping us identify trust breakdown she details methods and exercises to follow which can lead to repair. This is relevant not just to those in all kinds of work environments but to all of us in family and personal relationships also.*"
—Louise Doran, Managing Director, Creative Theatre Experience

"*Team trust is crucial and essential to get the job done at every level of group dynamics--from high school student group problem solving, to warfighter interaction in a flight of fighter aircraft. Without trust and teamwork, everything falls apart. When trust fails, how do you get it back? Read Trust Repair to get your team back on track and working to accomplish the mission.*"
—Dave Gibson, Northwest Youth Leadership Conference Director and Air Force Pilot, CINC MOWW, Col, USAF (Ret)

TRUST REPAIR

It IS Possible!

Proven Strategies to Help
Groups Get Unstuck

Wendy Fraser, Ph.D.

Archway Publishing books may be ordered through booksellers or by contacting:

Archway Publishing
1663 Liberty Drive
Bloomington, IN 47403
www.archwaypublishing.com
1 (888) 242-5904

ISBN: 978-1-4808-7108-3 (sc)
ISBN: 978-1-4808-7109-0 (hc)
ISBN: 978-1-4808-7107-6 (e)

Library of Congress Control Number: 2019902349

Print information available on the last page.

Archway Publishing rev. date: 7/10/2019

In honor of every person who believes that broken trust can be repaired. To your courage, hope, and commitment to build a better future.

"Peace does not mean an absence of conflicts; differences will always be there. Peace means solving these differences through peaceful means; through dialogue, education, knowledge; and through humane ways."

The Dalai Lama

CONTENTS

INTRODUCTION

If there is no trust, there is nothing.
Trust is all.

—Rob Thurman

Clear signs of tension and fatigue weighed heavily in the eyes and faces looking at me when I sat down to meet with them for the first time. I took a deep breath to center myself as a palpable undercurrent of fear and discomfort moved through the room and manifested through rigid and contorted body positions. Sitting back from the table, heads slightly turned away, their arms and legs were crossed so tight it was doubtful whether this group would let anything in, figuratively or literally. And yet, I was there to represent hope. Hope for something better than what they were all currently experiencing.

What follows next is a story, one of many I have experienced, about a group of ordinary people who lost trust in each other, found themselves stuck, and had to make an intentional choice about repairing trust. While conventional thinking suggests that trust is impossible to fix, these ordinary people were ready to alleviate the pain from the transgressions but were uncertain how to go about it and questioned whether it was even possible. They chose to give trust repair one last chance.

If there is one thing that I have learned from all my years of experience in coaching groups through trust repair, it is this: *it is often our mindset and beliefs about whether people can change that either ignites forward momentum or prevents us from trying.* This shift in mindset may appear to be a small step, but it is absolutely critical. This book is designed to help guide you to make the small, intentional steps toward trust repair. As you read the following story, be mindful that what may appear to be small steps are, in fact, not small at all.

———

When I stepped through the door to a remote satellite office of a large health insurance company and met the team of fourteen employees I would be working with over the next several months, I found them steeped in turmoil and utter frustration, and in a state of near hopelessness. Over the course of two years the level of trust within the group had fallen significantly. Blaming others, emotional outbursts, outright sabotage, and poor work quality plagued the office. Although many dreaded coming to work, they still cared deeply about their special purpose within their community, and it was this common thread of meaningful work that gave them resolve to try, once more, to mend relationships. They liked what they did; they just stopped trusting each other.

When we first began the work of repairing trust, the group felt they were making little progress. As one person put it, they felt like they were "merely listening to each person share their story again." While they might have felt they heard the stories before, this new setting and process provided the opportunity to listen to the experience with openness and empathy. Listening to these stories provided important clues as to why the group was so stuck. This work uncovered key trust-eroding experiences that were never fully resolved. The group needed adequate time to unpack and understand each person's perspective. As they listened to the impact of a given situation, they discovered misunderstandings and misinterpretations and slowly began to realize they all made mistakes and hurt each other without knowing it. Acknowledging the pain, whether it was intentional or not, began the process of repairing trust within the group.

Before these conversations took place, people were pointing

fingers at each other, but after much discussion, they began to realize they all played a part in the demise of trust. They realized they could all do something to improve it, and this realization ignited them. They began to learn the value of being curious, asking questions, and not allowing assumptions to fester. They also learned to give direct feedback and check in on each other's intentions.

At the conclusion of our work together, they were finally able to create new communication patterns, adjust decision-making authorities, and strengthen interpersonal relationships by having honest and meaningful conversations. They chose to leave the drama behind, slowly began to move forward, and even started to have fun at the office. If you were to visit this group today, you would have never thought there was once a time when they could not be in the same room without exploding into arguments. It was nothing short of extraordinary.

▬ ▬ ▬

I have many more trust repair stories just like this one. I know it is possible for groups to repair trust because I have conducted and gathered extensive research, personally lived it, and successfully coached groups through it. This body of work, which culminates in a repair model and trust framework, is designed to be informative and provide practical solutions. The tools included in this book also serve as a quick reference for immediate use.

As evidenced in the story above, when trust is violated, the road to repair can appear so daunting that, if left unattended, people will become dissatisfied with their jobs and begin operating at less than their capacity. Unresolved trust violations fester and start to overwhelm minds and hearts. Human beings cannot sustain such a heavy and burdened existence without the stress eventually taking its toll.

Now imagine if leaders and groups were equipped with the knowledge, skills, and support to strengthen relationships and, when necessary, remedy their own trust issues. Instead of thinking it is impossible, what if we believed things *could* improve? What if we knew *how* to repair trust and strengthen relationships? On top of that, what if I told you it can be done without individuals having to change who they are at their core? I know it is possible because I have personally witnessed it. I am sharing the exact step-by-step process and proven research-based strategies I used to help groups get unstuck so that you can do it, too.

The information presented in this book is not just for groups that are stuck. As a business consultant I have shared the trust behaviors model and tools with leaders and employees of well-functioning groups to strengthen their understanding of how to support healthy work relationships. As one manager put it, "I wish I had this trust information when I *first* started out as a supervisor. It would have helped me be a better leader *earlier* on in my career!" Whether you are just starting out supervising others or are a seasoned leader, there is always something to learn about how to keep a work group productive and satisfied. Employees can also benefit from the information contained in this book by learning about trust behaviors and strengthening relationships so that they can take an active role in improving their work environment.

All groups experience situations that are challenging. Human beings make mistakes and are fallible. These mistakes and missteps strain trust. While it may seem difficult, trust can be strengthened through intentional repair efforts. By integrating formal research with an extensive ten-year analysis of consulting client data, I discovered new truths about the nature of trust, how trust is broken, and how to impact repairs.

In addition to the assessments and tools provided in this book I have also included several real-life examples of client groups and organizations who were able to identify unhealthy trust issues and worked successfully to repair trust. Each of these examples serves as a reminder of the power of people's intellect, heart, and perseverance. I also examined the characteristics of groups that were unable to repair broken trust. As hard as they tried, their barriers were too steep to overcome.

I am an optimist. I believe that people can change if they want to. I believe that the structure of groups can provide the support and safety net to do the deep work and repair relationships. I have also been let down, disrespected, humiliated, and hurt by some of my own groups, and as much as I tried we did not repair trust. Sometimes, despite our best efforts, trust repair does not work. But I still believe trust is worth attempting to repair because, more often than not, we can make a positive difference in relationships. I am not implying that this model is foolproof and always produces the desired results, but if you embrace the research and exemplify the core behaviors explained in the model, you will expand your personal awareness, which will ultimately effect positive change.

Costs of Unresolved Broken Trust

I often hear people complain that it is too difficult or painful to try to repair trust, and I can understand why. Facing someone you believe wronged you is a perilous proposition. You may not want to open yourself up to vulnerability, and yet you would like the situation resolved. Sometimes I hear people say that it is the other person's fault and therefore the *other* person should change, initiate the first steps toward resolution, or make amends. What usually follows this dialogue is "But what if the *other* person will not change?" Should you remain stuck? Should you let it go?

What is the cost of unresolved trust violations on individuals? Foremost is the cost of individual's emotional well-being and physical health. There are impacts on the human body when people experience stress or hold on to resentment.[1] It ages you, it can adversely affect your immune system, and can wreak havoc on your physical body. Headaches, digestive problems, backaches, and neck aches are known side-effects. People in broken trust situations describe feeling less motivated, have decreased self-esteem, and appear more helpless. They feel they cannot affect the situation, so why bother? When people feel powerless, they tend to give up.

It is normal for groups to experience ups and downs. Not everyone gets along, and sometimes opinions clash, but overall individuals can work through these challenges. Trust, however, is different from the day-to-day ups and downs because trust is so emotionally laden. It invokes a visceral experience and intensifies the situation. The residue of trust violations becomes embedded in morale and employee engagement because people remember these incidents for years.

What is the cost of unresolved trust violations on organizations? Costs are incurred on multiple levels: human connectivity, productivity, service to customers, and results. Low trust or broken trust adversely impacts group effectiveness and organizational well-being. In the latest update of the *State of the American Workplace*, Gallup reported that only 33 percent of American workers are engaged at work.[2] While it is unclear how much disengagement is due to unresolved broken trust, it is clear from my research that trust issues are definite contributors to engagement and organizational well-being.

There is another important consequence of broken trust. It shows up in policies, procedures, roles, expectations, and how we get our work done. Many laws, rules, and regulations are created in reaction to broken trust. If mistakes are made at work, rules may be enacted that add oversight to ensure it does not happen again. Hospitals continuously revise processes to prevent mistakes and are highly sensitive to repairing trust between patients and healthcare professionals. Government is full of bureaucratic processes and steps, the existence of which often stem from an unfortunate or unfair event. Elected officials respond to these by passing new laws to repair trust with citizens.

Financial and Organizational Costs of Broken Trust

Over the course of my ten-year study on trust I asked participants to describe the specific costs of not repairing trust within their groups. Lauren,* an employee at a large university, reported that it

---

* All names and some facts have been changed to protect identities of all people.

cost a couple hundred thousand dollars plus the cost of using an outside contractor to fix equipment that was not installed properly after members of her team assured her that they had checked the equipment. George, a former member of a county maintenance team, described $2.5 million in equipment failures that he believed was directly tied to the trust issues he and his team experienced. If coworkers had communicated better, and if his boss had been open to people on his team giving him feedback, costly equipment failures may have been avoided.

Other study participants described these costs to unresolved trust:

- Loss of customers and market share
- Wasted time at work because people were talking about the low-trust experiences rather than work
- Loss of financial investors, donors, and sponsors
- Doing work over again, resulting in lost time and use of inventory supplies
- Increased mistakes and process delays
- Lawsuits filed
- Turnover of people, costing time to hire and train replacements
- Employee illness and sick days used
- Useless staff meetings because people do not talk or exchange ideas
- Lower morale and employee satisfaction
- Reduction of innovation and creativity

It's about Choice

I believe that people have the capacity to adjust their style, behavior, and mindsets to get along better with others and produce quality work. I believe this is a choice. It is *their* choice. We cannot make another person change or adjust their way of being no matter how hard we try, nor can we make someone acknowledge their impact on others, admit mistakes, improve their reliability, or honor their word. The only thing we can do is change ourselves or adjust our style, approach, and mindset in relationship to them. The only person we can change is ourselves. If we choose to let pain or anger about broken trust fester, we hurt ourselves. This can become all-consuming and can be continually relived.

According to sociologist Martha Beck, repeatedly telling a scornful story lights up the brain's pathways of suffering.[3] We are essentially experiencing the tragedy (trust violation) repeatedly. Believe me, when I talk with some people about trust violations, some describe such painful stories. Sometimes I am astonished by the time elapsed since the violation occurred. One man shared an experience with me that happened sixteen years earlier, and he described the events as if they happened yesterday. I could see the pain on his face and in his voice. Holding on to these experiences takes a huge toll. There is emerging research about rewiring your brain through adjusting your beliefs and self-talk. Telling yourself a different story could create new neural pathways and a new reality for you.

Intentions of This Book

I hope that you feel motivated to learn about repairing trust and explore the many tools and models designed to help you. This book is for leaders, facilitators, and team members who want to strengthen relationships and influence trust repair in groups. There are a few ways to use this book:

1. If you find yourself in a state of frustration or despair related to trust violations, this book can support you in knowing you have a choice in how you engage in repairing trust, and I offer tools to help you act on your choice.

2. If you are part of a group or partnership that is stuck or overwhelmed by unhealthy dynamics related to broken

trust, I provide suggestions for how you can move forward in an intentional, healthy way.

3. If you are a leader or practitioner, I offer proven strategies and tools to help you facilitate repairing trust and strengthening relationships between people and within groups.

How This Book Is Organized

Chapter 1 offers definitions and foundational information on trust. While there is not a singular definition of *trust*, it is helpful to embrace one that reflects a group perspective.

Chapter 2 offers a Trust Behaviors Framework that connects a comprehensive and systemic set of interrelated behaviors and actions that can be used as a guide to strengthen trust or as a self-assessment to identify areas for improvement.

Chapter 3 offers the Trust Repair Model. It provides an overview of practical steps group members can take to repair trust.

Chapters 4–7 delve into each phase of trust repair providing vivid descriptions, supportive narratives, and tools for immediate use.

Chapter 8 offers reflection on the research and demonstrates distinctions between the groups that successfully repair trust and those that do not.

Chapter 9 offers strategies for repairing trust when others may not be willing participants.

Chapter 10 offers resources and further exploration of the many facets of repairing trust. It includes ideas for leaders, facilitators, and group members.

Summary

Low trust, distrust, and unresolved trust violations leave people in a less than optimal state. Over time, these unresolved situations lead to both human and organizational illness. I am not about to tell you this is going to be an easy road, but if you are stuck in the trust mire and want out, there are strategies to help.

Repairing trust is hard work. It takes time and intentionality. This is where hope and positive thinking become crucial to the process. I believe in the resilience of the human spirit and that deep within our DNA we are wired to stay connected with other people. I have witnessed acts of forgiveness and group perseverance to work through messy issues enough times to know that it is possible to successfully repair trust in groups.

Interested in learning how? Read on.

CHAPTER 1
The Foundations of Trust

There is a common belief that once trust is broken it can never be fixed. Yet, that has not stopped people from attempting to repair it.

Nearly all aspects of daily life depend on trusting others, whether we are conscious of it or not. Purchasing food, seeking health care advice, driving to work, educating children, banking—almost all decisions involve trusting someone else. The more complex the society, the greater the dependence on others, and if trust weakens, the social order collapses.[1] If people lose trust in others, it affects how work gets done and how people communicate, problem-solve, and interact.

Trust is the thread that connects people and systems and what creates interdependencies. It permeates human interactions and operational systems and can serve as a catalyst for organizational and personal growth.

We need a balanced view of trust. Having 100 percent trust in others is not always a good thing. It can be too risky or naïve to extend trust too far and too quickly; therefore, some level of distrust may actually be healthy. Given the complexity of trust and relationships, there is room for both trust and distrust. It is why we have passwords on our internet accounts and banking systems. It is why I make my teenage daughter tell me where she's going. I trust her judgment and believe she's a great person, but she is still learning about life. As parents, her father and I need to provide healthy boundaries. So, we ask that she check in, and we give her a curfew. Having a healthy balance of distrust supports trust. Picture the volume dial of a stereo. Sometimes it makes sense to turn it up, and other times it is prudent to dial it down. Trust is not static, and each person chooses when and how to dial it up or down, depending on the circumstances.

> *Trust is the thread that connects people and systems and what creates interdependencies.*

Trust Starts Early

Adult development expert Erik Erikson suggests that our earliest seeds of trust are formed in the first eighteen months of life. Imagine an infant crying out for food, love, attention, and their caregiver or parent tending to the need. This infant experiences *"If I need something, I can rely on others to help me."* Now imagine another infant crying out for its basic needs but not satisfied fully, in a timely manner, or even kindly. This infant experiences *"If I need something, I cannot rely on others, so I must try to learn to take care of myself."*

According to Erikson's theory of personality development, the ego goes through stages as it successfully resolves crises that are distinctly social in nature. The earliest stage focuses on trust. "Trust v. mistrust (birth to 18 months). The infant looks to a primary caregiver for stability, consistency, predictability, and reliability of care. If the infant finds those qualities, a sense of trust is developed that carries into other relationships. The virtue sought in this stage is *hope*. When crisis arises, there is a real possibility people will be there to support. Failure to acquire hope leads to the development of fear."[2]

As people progress in life from infancy through adolescence and into adulthood, many experiences shape their ability to trust other people. Some, if their experiences have been positive, may tend to trust others first until shown otherwise. For others, trust comes only after other people have proven their ability to be trustworthy.

Everyone has a lifetime of experiences that shape their trust *story*. Where and how the person grew up, personality predisposition, cultural background, education, spiritual beliefs, racial, gender, and sexual identities, and adult development (maturity level) all influence a person's ability and willingness to trust. These become part of one's personal trust story. The complicated nature of individual development means that we cannot know the stories that are shaping others' conclusions about what is trustworthy, what they are willing to fight for, or what they can let go. What may be considered an egregious act that warrants immediate broken trust by some may be viewed as a nonissue by others. This is what makes working with people both interesting and confusing.

Reflection Questions

1. What is your trust story?
2. What have been the pivotal experiences in your life that shape and impact how, when, and why you trust others?
3. What beliefs do you hold as a result of these experiences?

What Is Trust?

There are many definitions of trust. After reviewing dozens of scholarly and practical definitions, I have adopted a variation of the Oxford dictionary description by adding the concepts of

Trust is a belief in the character, ability, reliability, and intentions of others and the willingness to risk vulnerability with them.

vulnerability and willingness to risk, because there is an emotional component in deciding whether or not to trust others. My working definition of trust for this book is *Trust is a belief in the character, ability, reliability, and intentions of others and the willingness to risk vulnerability with them.*

Trust is built or erodes through experiencing each other's character and actions. The most critical time frame for group members to develop trust is at the beginning of their relationship. Integrity demonstrated early in the relationship will be the most salient indicator of trust.[3] Examples of integrity that inform opinions about a person's character include honoring confidentiality, being truthful, and doing the right thing. If trust violations happen early in the relationship, before people can get to know each other's character, then the likelihood of engaging in trust repair is lower. They are not invested enough in the relationship with the other person.

The reverse is also true. If trust violations occur later in the relationship, there is a stronger probability that people will attempt to repair it because they have had more time to work together and build connections. They know each other better and may consider how each person's work patterns and personality style contributed to the violation of trust.

It is natural for groups to experience challenges and setbacks. If the challenge threatens trust, then the group must decide whether to engage in understanding what happened and either try to fix it or ignore it. If it is an overt breach of trust, then it is definitely something that needs fixing. Otherwise, if left alone, unresolved trust violations will likely hurt the individual's and the group's ability to be effective.

Repair occurs when the trust violation is remedied to the satisfaction of the people involved. The repair does not necessarily mean the group achieves its pre-violation trust level again. That may not be possible.

Repair occurs when the trust violation is remedied to the satisfaction of the people involved.

Imagine picking up the pieces of a broken mirror and trying to put it back together. Even if you carefully put every small piece back together, there will still be broken lines. You can look at the mirror and only see the cracked edges that remind you that the mirror was damaged. Or you can choose to look at the reflection beyond the lines staring back at you. Trust is like this mirror. When trust has been violated, people are not likely to forget it. You make a choice to see only the cracks, or you can recognize they are there and intentionally see the reflection the mirror is showing you, noticing the lines but making a choice not to be held back by the flaws.

Repairing trust takes time, intentionality, and tenacity. You must believe that you have something to gain by engaging in repair activities. Your hope of something better will be your source of inspiration and is crucial to this process.

Repair versus Restore

I use the word *repair* intentionally. To repair something is to make it workable again. I do not use the word *restore*. It is impossible to restore trust to its pre-violation condition. Why? People within the group and the group itself have changed due to experiencing the initial trust violation and then how they handled it. Trust may never be the same, but it can be just as good or even better after working through the repair process.

Violations

Trust violations carry more weight in our judgment of character than do trust-building actions. Violations include broken promises, unfounded accusations, hurtful behaviors, spreading of rumors, and not honoring confidentiality. Research shows that there is a tendency for people to explain away their own trust violations (e.g., due to external reasons) but at the same time to hold their co-workers

morally responsible for their trust violations.[4] People judge themselves by their intentions, which they can provide reasons to support, and yet they judge others by the impact of their actions. Here
is an example that reinforces this concept:

> Elaine: We shared some confidential personnel in-
> formation in our small management team. It was
> very important that the information not get out
> until a designated time. We all agreed. A few days
> later, staff asked us about rumors they were hearing.
> I figured out who shared the information. When I
> confronted my fellow manager, all she said was that
> she didn't mean to do it and it just slipped out. But
> I didn't buy it. When I probed more, she believed
> she had good reasons to share information with one
> person who would be most affected by the plans be-
> ing discussed. She knew the person had medical is-
> sues and needed uninterrupted insurance coverage.
> This manager meant well and wanted to support
> that person but didn't realize the impact her actions
> would have on the group.

Understanding trust violations will help you diagnose, strategize, and treat the situation. According to researchers A. R.
Elangovan and D. L. Shapiro, there are three types of violations:
accidental, opportunistic, and premeditated (intentional).[5] The key
to understanding the type of violation is the presence of intent
(what were people really thinking and wanting to do) and the timing
of actions.

- **Accidental violations:** The absence of intent is an accidental violation. This is where the person has no intention of
  violating the expectations or breaking trust with another
  person or the group. Accidental violations are sometimes
  seen as mistakes, and people often feel bad for it happening

in the first place and are quick to apologize for it once they become aware of it. Accidental violations can occur when people are new to their job positions. They make mistakes because they are learning how to do the work. It is easier to forgive someone for an error or a trust violation if they did not know how to do something in the first place.

- **Opportunistic violations:** These violations are the most frequent. They occur when an opportunity comes up and the person acts on it either without thinking about or paying little attention to breaking trust. Opportunistic violations can also be the result of poorly designed and/or executed policies and procedures. For example, when a procedure requires that two people count money and yet only one is counting the cash and might decide to pocket some, this can become an opportunistic violation. If the violation reoccurs, it becomes an intentional violation of trust.

- **Premeditated (Intentional) violations:** These are planned with an intent to commit a violation of trust. Bernard Madoff's Ponzi scheme fits this category. It is the result of a self-serving, deliberate action that benefits that person while undermining and hurting others. Intentional violations center on character and integrity. It is very difficult, though not impossible, to successfully engage in efforts to repair trust following intentional violations. It will require a lot of work and commitment to repairing the relationship when trust has been deliberately violated.

Psychological Safety

Google conducted a large study on the characteristics of high-performance teams. One critical piece of data that emerged in their results was the need for psychological safety in groups.[6] It makes sense. When people put forth ideas or ask questions, will they be accepted and explored? Or will they be shut down, ridiculed, shamed, embarrassed, or ignored? It is worth noting that when any one person is treated this way, everyone notices, and the group tends to shut down. Like trust, it only takes an instant to destroy psychological safety, and it takes many positive interactions to rebuild it. Everyone is responsible for it, not just the person leading the group.

Psychological safety is a vital component of group trust. Amy Edmondson defines psychological safety as a shared belief that the team is safe for interpersonal risk-taking. It is a belief system about how others will respond when reporting mistakes, offering ideas, or being vulnerable. She studied teams in three different environments (operating room teams, production, and new-product development management) and found that groups with higher levels of psychological safety were more likely to report errors and learn from them.

> "Psychological safety is a shared belief that the team is safe for interpersonal risk taking. It is a belief system about how others will respond when reporting mistakes, offering ideas, or being vulnerable."
> —Amy Edmondson

Edmondson also found that when rolling out organization-wide change initiatives, teams with higher levels of psychological safety were more likely to support the change initiatives and find ways to make it work. According to her research, five factors increase the chances of intact work groups having stronger psychological safety: leadership behavior (e.g., being accessible, modeling), trusting and respectful interpersonal relationships, practice fields (a place to practice and learn skills), organizational context support (e.g., access to resources and information), and emergent group dynamics.[7]

Organizations and groups with healthy psychological safety find increased risk-taking and innovation, which leads to stronger performance. They also have more resilient people who have a positive effect on morale, which also leads to stronger performance.

While leaders play a significant role in the creation of

psychological safety within their organizations, every person contributes as well. Group members cannot remain silent if another member is acting in a way that is diminishing the psychological safety in the group. For example, if you witness someone bullying another person, you must say something; otherwise, your silence magnifies the situation. You may feel uneasy about speaking up, but you must make a choice to make things better. If the situation were reversed, you would want others to speak up for you.

Leaders Heavily Influence Group Trust

Trust building, maintenance, and repair are heavily influenced by the nature of leadership that is present and how managers manage. I recognize that leadership and management are two different functions, and both play an important and symbiotic role in organizational effectiveness. However, for simplicity, I will use the word *leader* to describe both roles, even though each function has unique responsibilities. Similarly, I understand the differences between employees, volunteers, community members, and team members, but I will use the term *employee* flexibly throughout my writing. My hope is that you can translate that word into the appropriate role within your group.

The stakes for violating trust are more significant higher up in the organizational hierarchy. Leaders' actions impact the lives of their employees. One study of hierarchical relationships in groups illustrated that, because of their greater dependence and vulnerability, individuals in lower-status positions experience trust concerns more strongly.[8] Perception of any trust violation lasts longer and feels more poignant at the worker or team member level. An individual's status within an organization also plays a significant role in his or her willingness to engage in trust repair activities because it requires more courage and risks more vulnerability to challenge a superior on trust violations. Why? Leaders hold power over promotions, work assignments, and general conditions of employment.

A leader's character is important. Employees appraise the leader's character using terms like *integrity*, *fairness*, and *reliability*, and these influence the employee's work performance and mindset. Each interaction provides information about a leader's character and an employee's attempt to draw inferences about that leader's intent and personal nature.[9]

Turnover, employee satisfaction, customer satisfaction, and production data are all influenced by the level of trust in leaders and the work environment. Clearly, having the right people in these positions matters. People may be selected for leadership positions because they are very good technicians, but some of these people may not possess the competencies to build trust and lead people. They may have built trust in their technical skills, but they also need to build trust in their interpersonal and leadership skills. Some may need time to develop these skills and competencies.

I worked with a client for a few years who had repeatedly low employee satisfaction ratings and sought my help with trust repair. I remember a conversation with two leaders who were talking about a supervisor whose staff were miserable and whose unit was experiencing higher turnover than normal. These leaders tried for a few years to coach this supervisor. They sent him to training, provided him coaching and mentorship, and set clear expectations about how they wanted him to work with his team. The supervisor was an incredibly talented systems architect and couldn't stay out of the details of the projects his employees worked on. He often told them to do it again or revise plans to mirror the way he would do them. A self-proclaimed introvert, he disliked holding meetings and preferred to communicate with short, concisely worded emails. Additionally, he had clear rules around starting and ending times of the day and held his employees to more strict standards than the rest of the company.

After listening to leaders bemoan the situation, I asked if they were going to make a change and release this person from supervising others. The two leaders were surprised, maybe annoyed, that I had even posed the question. They claimed that they were going to continue to support the supervisor and do whatever they needed to help him succeed because that was what they believed good leaders should do—support their team. I asked, after three years of working to help him succeed, what other options could be explored to help this person find a great fit in the organization that did not include supervising people? Leadership is more expansive, and they needed to consider the effect on employees. I have found that if employees are miserable, work results can be adversely affected, which can lead to unhappy customers. I would like to say that this client made the change to remove the supervisor, but to my knowledge they did not. I believe fear about damaging his career or humiliating him outweighed disrupting the current situation, even though it was not working for the employees. What would have happened if that supervisor had been given the opportunity to do something else? It could have been a win-win, but fear of even entering the conversation left no winners.

On the other hand, leaders face difficulties as they attempt to build and maintain trust, even if they are good leaders. Leaders can face constraints because they are expected to work within the policies and cultural rules of the organization. Some of these may not support good communication and flexibility in decision-making, and therefore may adversely affect trust.[10]

For example, when dealing with a potential layoff, leaders usually agree to keep things confidential until all the details are finalized. Employees may ask about the impending change and whether they will be affected. As a result, leaders become torn between maintaining trust with peers working on the layoff situation and maintaining trust with employees, who value transparency and the truth.

My suggestion is to question the underlying belief system that you need to have all the details worked out before you can share things with your employees. Figure out what you can share and share it openly. Even if things change, then share what changed and move forward. People can handle changes if you keep them in the loop and doing so will improve the level of trust.

Summary

The nature of trust is complex and unique to each person. It is good to know your own story of experiences that shape your decisions around trust because it gives insight into what you deem trustworthy and what violates your trust in others. Trust is a belief in the character, ability, reliability, and intentions of others and the willingness to risk vulnerability with them. Trust becomes a thread that connects people and is an integral component of healthy relationships.

When a violation of trust occurs, it triggers many emotions and can adversely affect operations of a group. It is helpful to understand the root cause of the violation and determine whether it was accidental, opportunistic, or premediated (intentional). Trust violations always have an impact on the psychological contract between people, and that must be addressed if you are going to work through the successful repair of trust. Everyone in the group contributes and should tend to healthy psychological safety, not just leaders.

Leaders play an important role in trust repair and carry a heavier burden to work toward a healthy work environment. Make sure the right people are in leadership positions and that they are supported and well trained, even if it means moving people from supervisory responsibilities. Be mindful that it is not always easy for leaders to do their part because systems and organizational policies may influence their ability to build and maintain trust.

Repair occurs when the trust violation is remedied to the satisfaction of the people involved. It is possible to repair trust within groups, but it takes time, intentionality, and tenacity to do it successfully.

CHAPTER 2
Trust Behaviors Framework

You must trust and believe in people,
or life becomes impossible.
—Anton Chekhov

Before diving into the trust repair model, let us examine the kinds of behaviors that constitute trust. Over the past ten years, I gathered responses from nearly one thousand leaders, employees, sports team members, customers, and volunteers in all kinds of organizations.[1] I asked them to provide input regarding those behaviors that contributed to trust and those behaviors that caused low trust, distrust, and broken trust. As I reviewed their responses, themes emerged from this action research and informed my thinking. I built an assessment model to connect their input and created a trust behaviors framework specifically for groups and organizations. I am excited about the result for several reasons. It is grounded in leadership, organization development, systems, and group development theories, and it is based on real experiences from people like you.

This research shows that there are patterns of behaviors that support organizational effectiveness and trusting relationships. The trust behaviors are grouped in five categories: purpose, roles, core processes, communication, and interpersonal dynamics. I placed them in this order because of how each influences the next category. However, the behaviors within each category are not in any priority order because all the behaviors listed are important and contribute to healthy trust.

Trust Behaviors

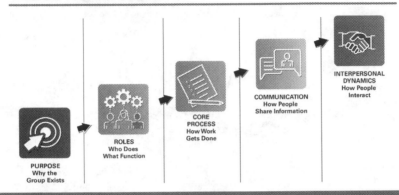

Behaviors that affect relationships in groups

The behavior categories are in order because of how each influences the next category.

The foundational part of the trust behaviors framework is the **Purpose** category. Clarity of purpose is first because all groups need to know why they exist and what purpose they are serving. If the reason for existence is unclear or the scope of a project is not well defined, it will have a drastic effect on people's understanding of their roles, how work gets done, communication, and how people interact.

The second category is **Roles**. If the purpose of a group or project is clear, then each person must understand their role in supporting that group mission or project purpose. People need to know their own role as well as understand the roles and responsibilities of other people in the group. Otherwise, if roles are not clear, people will not know how to accomplish the work assigned as well as they could.

CORE PROCESS
How Work Gets Done

The third category is **Core Process**, and it encompasses how work is designed and gets completed. You can expect trust problems in this category if either the purpose or the roles are not well defined. In a world where things change so quickly, there will be changes to core processes that can affect layers up and down the trust behaviors framework. How work gets done will certainly affect communication patterns and then how people treat each other.

COMMUNICATION
How People Share Information

The fourth category is **Communication**. Clear patterns of communication and decision-making help make the top three categories (purpose, roles, and core processes) run well. It is easy to misinterpret information, forget to include certain people, read meaning into messages, and mess up communications without intending to do so. Each missed opportunity for good communication affects trust.

INTERPERSONAL DYNAMICS
How People Interact

The final category is **Interpersonal Dynamics**. This is what people experience the most when trust is low and when there are problems in any of the other categories: purpose, roles, core processes, and communications. Interpersonal dynamics generate the most obvious symptoms (e.g., rudeness, dismissal, isolation), and it becomes the focus area that people want fixed first. But instead of focusing on team building as a remedy for the problems, you must begin considering how the foundational parts of the framework affect how people interact.

Purpose Trust Behaviors

PURPOSE
Why the
Group Exists

Purpose entails clarity about why the group or organization exists. Leaders may assign the purpose to the group, but group members are also responsible for understanding the purpose and working to achieve it. Any uncertainty will adversely affect the rest of the trust behavior categories. If people do not understand purpose, they may work unknowingly against it, eroding trust. To support a strong purpose in groups and organizations:

- Determine purpose, direction, scope, priorities, and boundaries
- Align people, systems, and resources for success

If you are unclear about the purpose of a group or organization, it will affect what you do to support it. If you are unclear about your role, it affects how work gets done because you are fuzzy about who is supposed to do what part. Communication patterns and interpersonal dynamics become symptoms because of the lack of clarity in the structural components at the top of this pyramid. Purpose and role clarification must be firmly in place to allow for operational effectiveness. This is why purpose is the first category of questioning when groups are stuck. If they are stuck at this level, there are likely problems and issues in all of the other categories.

Eighteen percent of the participants in my study described trust violations stemming from unclear purpose, scope, or misaligning people and resources. Here are two examples:

Fred: Whenever we came together to generate guidelines on how we were going to make decisions, we would discuss it a lot but never get anywhere. Eventually, we just came to the point where we couldn't spin anymore so we started moving forward without resolving the fundamental issues about the direction of the overall project. That was a big mistake.

Monique: For the very first time, the person at the head of the department did not know our business or really cared about it. And our work was changing significantly. For a few years, we were told to cultivate business partner relationships, and now we are being told to keep our distance from them. But the person at the top didn't know how big of an impact that would be to our business. We were just left with a 180 change and told to deal with it.

Strengthening Purpose-Level Trust

Determine Purpose, Direction, Scope, Priorities, and Boundaries

It truly starts here. Why does the group exist? What is the purpose of the group or organization? If a project team is formed, what are the boundaries of the work so they stay within scope? What should the focus be first? What are the priorities, and who gets to set them? The answers to these purpose questions are paramount for helping groups succeed.

Tools like team charters are a must for temporary or even ongoing teams to ensure understanding of their purpose. Despite teams and/or managers insisting that everyone knows why they exist and what they are expected to do, it is a mistake to make assumptions and overlook this necessary step. It is inevitable that at some point members will question the boundaries of the work and seek clarification from the sponsor. They end up spending more time later in the process by asking questions they should have had answered in the beginning. Or worse yet, without a charter, they risk going off task, and when the team finishes the work to their satisfaction, they face disappointment to find that the sponsor of that team will not implement the recommendations because they were out of scope. This is a surefire way to reduce people's enthusiasm in volunteering for future team projects.

Finally, organizations need clarity of purpose to support their strategic direction. Strategic plans need foundational mission, vision, values, and goals to help navigate decisions and operational plans. Clarity of direction and purpose build trust between organizational leaders and employees because they know where they are going.

Align People, Systems, and Resources for Success

Once the direction is set, leaders and managers must align the human and operational systems to accomplish the organization's purpose. Exploring ways to best align people and their talents should be a thoughtful task. People want to feel engaged in meaningful work. Aligning them with the purpose right away can support their connection to the overall organization, but it can also show your intentionality to find a best fit for their skills. Putting people in the right place at the right time is a critical leadership function. If you do these parts well, you build trust. If there is any mismatch between people's knowledge, skills, abilities, or attitudes with work assignments and organizational culture, trust will be affected.

However, alignment is more than just fitting people into the right places. People need appropriate resources so they can be successful. Systems need adjusting and consideration in the equation. If you are going in a new direction, do your systems (e.g., policies and procedures, technology, or human systems) reflect that? Spend the time to ensure the whole system is heading in the direction of your stated purpose.

Indicators of Problems with Purpose-Level Trust Behaviors

To sum up, when purpose is not clear, people may do things that are not aligned with the purpose. Indicators of problems with purpose that can lead to the erosion of trust include:

- Unclear scope of a project, mission of an organization, or purpose of a group leaving people feeling directionless and uncertain
- Fuzzy operational or project boundaries causing crossover into other departments or work processes
- Misalignment of people because the goal is not clear causing a mismatch of selecting the right people to work on the project
- Wasted time or resources because of uncertainty
- Little or no direction provided by leadership to employees
- Conflicting goals put people and resources at odds to compete for attention

Roles Trust Behaviors

ROLES
Who Does
What Function

The roles of each person in the group need to be fully understood by everyone in that group. Any fuzziness about who is supposed to do what task affects how work gets done, how people communicate, and how they interact. When people do not understand their role, they can step on other people's toes or not do what others expect of them. To support the roles of people in groups and organizations:

- Establish clear roles, responsibilities, mutual expectations, and accountability

- Set people up for success, delegate well, and create support systems
- Honor agreements, commitments, and confidentiality

Think about how often things change in groups and organizations. Roles shift as work evolves through technology updates and process improvements. You need to spend time adjusting roles and responsibilities to match direction or process changes. Violations of trust emerge when there is a mismatch of people's skills sets to the role, not just when roles are not clear. Can the responsible people do their jobs? Are they willing or unwilling to perform the basic job requirements?

Thirty-six percent of the broken or low-trust behaviors described by participants in my study centered on the roles and responsibilities of people. Here are some real experiences:

> Matthew: He was getting a lot of pressure from people inside (the team) for him to do his own share of the work. I don't think he could do the job. I think that was one of the biggest problems. There were performance targets and he had been underperforming. He wanted to be liked, but he was in a collections position. He would talk with people down the hall instead of doing his job. The co-workers in his unit were getting mad. I don't think his personality fit the position.

> Monique: Tamisha was handling a lot of the contracting and doing tons of work and Andre didn't understand how stressful that was for her. She wanted him to help with some of the paperwork (logistics, writing the contract, interoffice agreements), but he refused, stating it wasn't his role. Her perception was that he thought it was beneath him. It was clear that Andre had a completely different

perception of his role and Tamisha's role. This was the core trust issue between them.

Strengthening Role-Level Trust

Establish Clear Roles, Responsibilities, Mutual Expectations, and Accountability

Everyone deserves clarity about individual roles so that they can do their best to perform the work. Individuals need to know how the work they are doing supports the mission and overall purpose of the group, project, or organization. This is essential in aligning people and resources, so you accomplish your purpose. Everyone needs to understand and comprehend what is expected of them. People want to do their best, so take the time and clarify expectations, but be open to their input. You will strengthen trust by setting mutual expectations together. If these conversations are one-way, done poorly, based upon assumptions, or never initiated, you miss an important opportunity to build trust at a structural level. Finally, make sure you put people in the right positions to match their knowledge, skills, and abilities, because fit matters.

Set People Up for Success, Delegate Well, and Create Support Systems

As you consider individuals and their roles on your team, ensure that they have access to the information and resources necessary to successfully perform their jobs. Ensure they are properly trained, and create healthy support systems around your team members. You can help your team members develop support systems by discussing various people who can serve as role models, challengers, subject matter experts, and friends.

Finally, if you are giving people additional assignments, please do not do drive-by delegation. This means do not passively, casually, or quickly ask someone to take on a piece of work without taking the time to appropriately delegate. William Onken Jr. wrote a great article that related delegation to a concept he called "monkey management."[2] A task or piece of work is the monkey. If you want someone else to care and feed for this monkey, then you must ensure they know *how* to do it. Tasks involved in clear delegations (the caring and feeding of your monkey) include providing clear purpose of the work, who is supposed to do what, boundaries, budget and resource clarification, communication expectations, results, timelines, and what support is needed. When proper delegation does not occur, mistakes can happen, or work does not get completed as desired, leaving everyone frustrated.

Honor Agreements, Commitments, and Confidentiality

Do what you say you are going to do. Period. Honoring agreements and commitments impacts how people perceive you. If you have a lot on your plate and cannot get to everything, reach out and renegotiate with those with whom you have agreements and commitments.

I have learned the hard way on this one. Because I want to be of service, I tend to say yes to requests for my time, talent, and expertise. This can lead to trouble if I overextend myself. While managing everything on my plate, when competing deadlines emerged, I did my own version of triage and decided who got my time and others would just have to wait. By doing this, I eroded trust between myself and the other parties whom I decided could wait because I did not honor the deadlines (commitments and agreements). When faced with the challenges of competing commitments, the right thing to do is reach out to the parties and renegotiate. Any ability to adjust due dates? Can other people do what I am doing? What other adjustments can be made so I can manage the crunch? In reflecting on my pattern of overextending myself, I must get better at negotiating timelines and expectations. This, for me, is a work in progress. Just because I am aware of it does not mean it goes away. I must be intentional about negotiating realistic deadlines and expectations or let them know I just cannot help right now.

People who are perfectionists also need to negotiate timelines and commitments. To maintain trust, they must be intentional about managing deadlines so that they can still do their best work and have the extra time they need to make sure it is of excellent quality.

Leaders play a role in helping employees effectively honor agreements and commitments. How? By not overburdening the same people with committees, work requests, and other assignments. If you are in a leadership position, are you spreading opportunities around? This builds capacity and capability within your team. You may have some critical go-to people you call on for help. But you may be contributing to their stress by continuing to go to them and asking them to do things on top of their normal workload. Do you let them say no to you? What about asking other people?

It really matters who holds these leadership positions. Leaders directly impact the effectiveness of teams and organizations. There is reciprocal trust – they need to trust their employees to do their jobs well and support them with resources, appropriate authority, and growth opportunities. When leaders demonstrate support and trust to allow employees to do their jobs, employees can trust that their leaders are doing their jobs.

NOTE: These first two layers in the trust behaviors model, purpose and roles, comprise what I call "structural components" in organizations and groups. They must be solid and clear for people, otherwise they contribute to problems in the other categories (process, communication, and interpersonal dynamics). This was a major finding in my research study on trust repair in groups. While only some of my participants expressed structural issues as being a contributor initially, structural issues surfaced as having more of an impact than people realized. Remedies to improve trust needed to include structural clarification. It is the interpersonal dynamics that we feel first and want to fix. But the true fix needs to start at the top with purpose and roles.

Indicators of Problems with Role-Level Trust Behaviors

To summarize, when roles are not clear, people become confused and cannot be efficient in their work. Indicators of problems with roles that can lead to the erosion of trust include:

- Unclear roles and responsibilities for yourself or your fellow group members
- Poor delegation
- Little or no accountability or follow-through; people not owning their responsibilities
- Wasted time as people try to sort out who does what task
- Conflict as people do not know who is responsible for assignments
- Overburdened people
- Expectations not well managed, leaving people over- or underworked
- Information not shared between roles

Core Process Trust Behaviors

CORE
PROCESS
How Work
Gets Done

Core process refers to getting work done effectively to carry out the purpose of the work or organization. To maintain healthy trust, the core work of a group must be set up, managed, modified, and improved. It includes reliability and consistency factors and whether people can rely upon each other to do their parts in the work flow. Embedded in this category is whether employee input and engagement are effectively sought and used for the betterment of work processes and systems. If the core processes are not well defined, it could lead to inefficient operations and increased costs because it affects products and services as well as the relationships of the group members. To support strong core processes:

- Improve operations, relationships, and results; and be open to new ways of doing things
- Ensure consistency, reliability, and responsiveness
- Engage people, broadening decision-making, and ask for input

Sixty-one percent of the low-trust or broken trust behaviors described by participants in my trust study explain how work is initiated and completed through core processes. Here are some real examples of how core process-level trust adversely affected the group:

George: We had a system where we were each assigned a certain building to manage the requests and preventative maintenance. With this process, we knew that building very well and knew what maintenance it needed when. We had an informal system where people would send us emails if they needed something. We were all accountable for responding to these requests and did so with pride.

Things changed when our supervisor wanted more documented performance metrics. They got a new computer system to track requests, and it was supposed to tell us when things needed routine maintenance. It didn't work correctly, and it was telling us to perform preventative maintenance when it wasn't the right time. And when we tried to talk to our supervisor about it, we were told just to do it.

Joan: We were under very time-sensitive constraints. We used an outside group to help us with the survey data, but they were a couple of weeks late in getting the data back to us. A couple of weeks were a *huge* hit against our deadline. What we had was an insanely complicated model that had cutting-edge components, and in the end, we didn't meet our quality of work expectations. We now had to fix it and work on restoring our credibility with our client. We were embarrassed!

Strengthening Core Process—Level Trust

Improve Operations, Relationships, and Results; and Be Open to New Ways of Doing Things

When it comes to our work, nothing stays static. I have worked with continuous process improvement (Lean Six Sigma) methodologies for more than twenty-five years. How we work is a function of how leaders set up the processes and encourage openness to improving them. The core tenets of Lean principles are continuous improvement and respect. Respect the people working in the process. Improving our core work means being conscious of how our customers and stakeholders receive our products and services. Respect flows through the organization and is embedded in our core work. It is how we engage and manage relationships with each other. When we do this well, we improve our operations and results. Building trust within and outside our organization means keeping our processes relevant so they yield strong results. Trust is also built as we innovate, renew, and examine our processes. We must be open to new ways of doing things, including responses to these questions: Are we doing the right things? Should these things be continued? Who are we serving and what do they expect? So much can be gained by reviewing lessons learned after projects end and using these lessons to inform the next project.

Ensure Consistency, Reliability, and Responsiveness

How people perform the work and how the group performs play a big role in consistency and reliability. Is the quality of my work consistent? Can people count on consistency among members of my team if we hold similar positions? Am I reliable? Do I get my work done efficiently, correctly, and in a timely manner? Can you depend on me to do my part? Can I depend on you to do yours? If I say I am going to do something, do I follow through? Can I count on you to do the same? Responsiveness is a core trust behavior. If I ask you a question or need your help, will you be responsive to that request? Will your response be timely, thoughtful, and relevant? You can be consistent and do great work, but if you do not respond in a timely manner to requests, people will lose trust in you. If you cannot do something, then say so as soon as possible. This will strengthen reliability and responsiveness.

Engage People, Broaden Decision-Making, and Ask for Input

Another aspect of quality core process work is pushing decision-making out to the employees working in the process. Whenever you must stop and ask someone to decide on a course of action, such as requiring a supervisor's approval for a retail return or approve a license request, you slow down a process. What value is that signature and approval anyway? Why can't the criteria or considerations that the supervisor uses in the decision-making process be delegated to the employees working in the process so they can perform the whole process without interruption?

If you are tinkering with a process, you need input from the people who work with that process on a regular basis. Without such input, you risk process breakdown. People need to have a voice in shaping their core work. Do you want to silence voices and suppress inspiration? We need to unleash the creative talent and minds of people. Ask for their input. It builds trust and fosters a healthier and more productive environment, ultimately making you a stronger leader.

Indicators of Problems with Core Process—Level Trust Behaviors

When core processes are not clear, you run the risk of frustrated, confused, and inefficient employees and risk alienating your customers. Indicators of problems with core purpose that can lead to the erosion of trust include:

- Lack of documented procedures leading to inconsistencies in work
- Low standards or not meeting standard expectations for work outputs
- Little to no follow-through or responsiveness
- Poor work quality or rework, resulting in lost time and requiring additional resources to fix it
- Clashes about how work should be performed
- People feeling their input does not matter at work or feeling unsafe to give input

Communication Trust Behaviors

COMMUNICATION
How People
Share Information

Communication includes the nature, patterns, tone, methods, and intentions regarding how people share information, problem-solve, and make decisions. Personality styles heavily influence this category. For example, some people like giving and receiving detailed information, while others like the high-level abbreviated version. Some people trust data and information they can see, research, and experience themselves, while others trust their internal hunches and ability to make sense of disparate information points. One of the four continuums of the Myers-Briggs Type Indicator, a classic personality instrument, is dedicated to the way people prefer gathering information and its influence on what data sources they trust. If communication norms are not established, then people miss valuable information which can severely impact operations and strain relationships. To support healthy communication in groups and organizations:

- Listen openly without judgment or interruption, and tune in to the quiet voices
- Check in on assumptions, intentions, and mutual understanding
- Seek feedback, sound and current information, and new perspectives
- Share timely, relevant information; avoid surprises; and be transparent and truthful
- Foster curiosity and open-mindedness, and engage in healthy challenges to conventional thinking

Seventy-five percent of the teams described violations of trust involving communications. Here are some examples from this study:

> Tony: Initially, the Latin American business own-ers would send in the data, but they never knew if they (corporate) got it. No one would give them any feedback. So, they stopped sending it. After a while, when they would get a request from corporate for data, they would basically ignore it because they felt ignored, and that became a trust issue.

> Madi: About four months into the process, we found out that some of the information was getting out even though we signed a charter and agreed that when we rolled out the program we would roll it out to everyone at the same time. No advance warning to anyone. But information started to get back to us, which meant someone on our team broke our confidentiality agreement.

Strengthening Communication-Level Trust

Listen Openly without Judgment or Interruption, and Tune in to the Quiet Voices

Listening is an art and a science. It takes patience and skill to rest your quick-thinking mind and be fully present while listening to someone. One of the best messages around listening comes from journalist Celeste Headlee. I recommend that you watch her TED Talk (filmed in April 2015). I have used her precise eleven-minute talk with groups to reinforce points about good listening and good conversations. One of her key points is listening to people as if each person has something very exciting and unique about them, which is absolutely true for every individual. What a powerful reminder of letting someone know you care when you listen to their messages with interest, openness, and without interruption.

Here's another question: How are you tuning in to your quieter people – the introverts who process information inside their heads? Are you making the space for their voices in meetings or in private conversations? Take time in meetings to pause the conversations for thinking by asking people to think quietly for three minutes about something. Consider methods where you invite each person to comment and go around the group without interruptions. If there is nothing to add, your introverts will not mind saying that, but they will appreciate the opportunity for input.

Finally, one of my most difficult pieces of feedback came from a friend regarding how I interrupted her when she was speaking. I'll never forget that moment she let me know how disrespected she felt when I did it. I was crushed. I had no idea I was doing it. I apologized right away and told her it was never my intention to make her feel that her words were not important. Upon reflection, I realized I interrupted people quite often. People would talk, and as I listened, words came out of my mouth. It was my way of saying to them, unconsciously, that I was following their story and engaged.

But I realize that for some people, my words were not what they were going to say, and they had to get back on track. This was such powerful feedback for me, and I am grateful she gave it to me. Even though it was never intentional, I had an impact on her. I also realized that my family does this a lot. Some habits are hard to break, but we must work on it if we want to be in effective relationships with others.

One more thought on interrupting. We have been socialized to accept others interrupting us when there is a perceived power difference. For example, men interrupting and talking over women, or bosses interrupting employees, parents interrupting children. We need to be conscious of these socialized patterns and ask ourselves, *Is this the way I want to be treated? How can I become more aware of these patterns so that I don't have a negative impact on others?*

Check In on Assumptions, Intentions, and Mutual Understanding

Misunderstandings play a big role in the erosion of trust. Someone says something, and my brain interprets it. I make instant assumptions based on my history with the person, my mood, and so many other things. Am I assuming correctly? How about checking in on a person's intention? Yes, of course. But why don't we do this more often? How do we know if we have mutual understanding? Just thinking you do and then nodding your head does not mean you have mutual understanding or agreement. Take the time to get clear and check in.

When I first became a supervisor, I had a lot to learn. I made a huge mistake that could have ended with a very damaged relationship. My one and only employee turned in a mileage reimbursement request. I felt it was excessive for where she lived and where she attended the training. So, instead of asking her and checking in, I went to human resources to seek advice on what to do. They suggested I write a letter and present it to her so I could be clear about expectations. So, I did that. I wrote a letter, invited my employee to a meeting with the HR person, and read it. She was shocked. She left the meeting, and then a day later I was invited to a meeting with her and the same HR representative in attendance while I listened to her reply. She shared that she had taken the wrong route on her way to the training course. A simple mistake, one that I didn't ask her to explain in the first place. I felt terrible. But, I felt even worse when I realized how it must have made her feel when I surprised her with a formal letter and an HR witness. I apologized. We later spoke about the learning and created a code word for ourselves – code yellow—that if either of us used it, we would immediately stop what we were doing and find a private place to talk. We never did use the code word, but our relationship strengthened when I admitted my mistake and we actually talked like adults.

Seek Feedback, Sound and Current Information, and New Perspectives

Sometimes all it takes is one experience and we've generated our opinion, made decisions, and that's that. Making quick decisions can help in some situations. But making quick decisions can also backfire. How unfortunate, because what we really need is sound and current information. I often hear people say that they just know why people do things, what they are thinking or feeling, or that they know what their intentions were. That's interesting to me. How do you really know? We really cannot know what is true for other people. You must be open to listening and widening your perspectives. Ask questions. You do not have to have all the answers. In fact, asking more questions is better than having answers. Why? It keeps us fresh and continually learning.

When I hear people—managers especially—claim that they are surprised by feedback, it makes me curious. For example, when the annual employee satisfaction survey results are shared with managers and some say they are surprised by the data, it makes me think they aren't paying attention. If morale is low, there are many indicators expressing it even before a survey captures it. Feedback is always available in the system—which is the group or organization. Are you open to receiving it and understanding it? Do you specifically ask for feedback from others? Then, what do you do with it?

Finally, how open are you to new perspectives? If you are like most people, we tend to think we are very open. Opening yourself up to ideas that are different than your own takes skill, intention, and ego management. I teach people how to adapt to change. I work with Lean Six Sigma methodologies that encourage people to look at their work through the lens of customers and seek ways to improve. Yet, when my husband moved the tissue box from one side of the kitchen to the other without talking with me first I threw a fit. How's that for openness?

For years, the tissue box was on the counter next to the oven. It happens to be closest to the living room and whenever I need a tissue (cue tender scene on television causing Wendy to cry), I automatically got up and got one. But after John moved the tissue box closer to the sink, it annoyed me. I'd get up to get a tissue and the box wasn't there...*grrr!* My first instinct was to move the box back, and I did on a few occasions, only to find it moved back by the sink. When we finally had a conversation about it, I was not open to hearing his reasoning. I wanted the tissue box where it had always been because it worked for me. John's perspective was the tissue box was closer to the garbage can and sink so people can wash their hands after using and discarding it. Makes sense. I still grumbled about it though, but I have slowly accepted it. We are human and creatures of habit. Being open to new perspectives takes discipline and support. Let's all be there for each other with a little bit of humor when we are trying to embrace change...and maybe even a tissue!

Share Timely, Relevant Information; Avoid Surprises; and Be Transparent and Truthful

People need information to do their jobs well. It needs to be timely and relevant. Honor your word and be truthful. You demonstrate integrity by being honest and transparent. Now, I recognize that we must use some filters with our truth. If you have decency, you are not likely to tell Aunt Martha her turkey was dry and boring at Thanksgiving after she's worked all day on the meal. That may be your truth, but being open and transparent about it takes finesse if you still want to be invited back to the family meal table next year. You will have to figure out how to politely give feedback if she asks; otherwise, enjoy the meal and add more gravy.

When I work with teams who are formulating recommendations for others, I suggest a no-surprise policy. Consider a champion-level track relay team. They practice smoothly handing off the baton to each other. There is a dedicated track space for the handoff so both athletes can run at similar speeds when it happens. And all four athletes continue to stay engaged in the whole race by running, by cheering each other on, and by watching the other handoffs so that they can learn to do it better. And they practice a lot. This is brilliant.

Now apply the relay concept to teams generating recommendations. The recommendation is the baton. How often do teams ensure that each recommendation has a specific person to receive the handoff? Are they running at the same pace? Once I was invited to an executive meeting where a team was presenting their final improvement recommendations to their sponsor only to hear that two out of the five recommendations were for me to do something. This was a surprise to me. Using the relay metaphor, I felt like I was in the stands cheering on the athletes when one stops and throws me the baton. What? I was surprised to hear the recommendation, which was something as broad and unspecific as "improve communications in the organization." Really? Had I "run" with the team for a while before they got to their final presentation, I would have understood more about what they were trying to do. I would have been able to persuade (or influence) them to not create a recommendation that assigned one person responsible for ensuring that 1,200 people understood each other. Good grief, I keep trying to improve communications in my small family of four, and it is constant work!

Foster Curiosity and Open-Mindedness, and Engage in Healthy Challenges to Conventional Thinking

How do you normally react when people challenge you? Do you feel threatened, insulted, or anxious? Or do you welcome questions because it will help you think more clearly and explore different facets of the situation? Curiosity and open-mindedness are powerful strategies that strengthen relationships. By asking questions and staying open to the possibilities, you also avoid the risks that come with making wrong assumptions.

Indicators of Problems with Communication-Level Trust Behaviors

Many communication issues contribute to the erosion of trust:

- Withholding information or sharing only partial truths
- Making assumptions without checking in for more sound and current information
- Not honoring confidentiality agreements
- Interrupting or not listening to people
- Close-mindedness and not being open to or asking for different perspectives
- Lack of timely or complete information

Interpersonal Dynamics Trust Behaviors

INTERPERSONAL
DYNAMICS
How People
Interact

Interpersonal dynamics are affected by every category layer above and influence how people interact with each other. With trust issues, we tend to experience the interpersonal dynamics first even though problems likely started in the layers above: purpose, roles, core processes, and communication. What people feel most are the tensions from the interpersonal dynamics, such as rude, snarky, or bullying behaviors.

These impede good communications and can interfere with productivity, so we want those fixed first because we *feel* them in a more significant way. That is why consultants are hired to do team building, when more diagnostic work is needed to understand the source of the issues first. If people are not getting along because they are not clear about who is supposed to do what, role clarification is needed before team building. This is a reason why team building can fail, because it is being used to treat the symptoms of other issues. Behaviors that support healthy interpersonal dynamics include:

- Model high standards, integrity, and vulnerability
- Invest in the growth and development of others
- Acknowledge mistakes and your impact on others and sincerely apologize in a timely manner
- Strengthen relationships and connectivity by investing time and energy into building others up, and avoid gossip, which erodes self-esteem and group connectivity
- Respect people's unique contributions, honor different perspectives and styles, and be inclusive and welcoming

Eighty-nine percent of the participants in my study described trust violations around interpersonal dynamics. It's not surprising that most people described how they treat each other as the number one indicator of eroding or broken trust. Here are some examples:

> Carol: And this manager was brutal. She came in one day and stood over my assistant's desk and almost beating her said, "I need this! Hurry up! Hurry up, you are not doing this fast enough!" She was doing this to all of us.

> Richard: This person was like a drive-by shooter. He shot rude comments as he walked by.

Strengthening Interpersonal Dynamics-Level Trust

Model High Standards, Integrity, and Vulnerability

People watch each other and mentally keep track about how you treat others, your integrity, your work standards, and so on. Does your work reflect high standards? Do you do the right thing even if no one is watching? Do your words match your actions? Do you let your human side show to others? Showing vulnerability is not weakness. Being your true, authentic, and vulnerable self encourages others to do the same. When we are vulnerable with each other, it strengthens connectivity, empathy, and understanding, and we can more readily accept feedback from each other.

Invest in the Growth and Development of Others

Give people opportunities to stretch their skills and take on new tasks. Offer them chances to serve on committees, team projects, and other special assignments. Spread these roles around to different folks and not just the same people. Ask team members what they want to learn and how they want to grow. Do not limit others' growth potential by deciding their capacity or interest for them. Partner with them, but remember that everyone is responsible for their own growth and development. However, we each can play a role in supporting and investing in it.

One of my most memorable bosses, who was affectionately called Yoda, used a metaphor when he stretched us beyond what we thought we could do. He said he was in a boat and had a life jacket for us whenever we struggled with a work challenge. He believed that to grow, we sometimes need to take on a bit of water to show ourselves that we can muster the courage and strength to accomplish the goal. He rarely overreacted and had an inordinate amount of patience. He had full faith that we would somehow "get it," even if we had doubts about our abilities. He was intentional about the growth and development of others, and he was also a life ring there to support us every step of the way.

Acknowledge Mistakes and Your Impact on Others, and Sincerely Apologize in a Timely Manner

In my trust study, 92 percent of groups that did not repair trust did not acknowledge that the violations of trust had an impact on others. Think about it. Through direct action or inaction, there is *always* an impact on others. People are hungry for acknowledgment that pain occurred because of those actions. Whether it was intentional or not, people must be willing to acknowledge their part and the impact it had on others, or trust cannot be fully repaired.

Managers who allow employees to blame and not acknowledge impact on others also violate trust. Accountability builds trust. People unwilling to admit mistakes may be an indication of an unsafe workplace.

In addition, my study data illuminated the problem of admitting mistakes and apologizing. In every team experience where they were unable to repair trust together, no one apologized if an apology was needed. We seem to live in a "whatever" society: if I do something that affects you, it is *your* problem, and I will not acknowledge or apologize for my actions. Ego, pride, and self-protection feed and reinforce people's notions that their version of the facts is correct. No wonder groups struggle with repairing trust.

Mistakes can be embarrassing, and admitting them to others can be difficult. Own your mistakes, learn from them, and make things right. Avoid the urge to rush past mistakes, or you might not get the learning. Learn to sit with the experience. Sometimes our feelings of embarrassment are so overwhelming that we will do anything to minimize or forget the mistake.

I am not talking about gushing over the mistake and throwing yourself on a sword. No need for that. Here's an example of a mistake that I compounded because of my embarrassment. Last year, I was digitizing my DVD collection onto a hard drive so that I can take my movies and watch them when I travel. One night we rented two movies, and I had a short debate in my head about copying those onto my hard drive (cue the integrity debate: am I doing the right thing?). I knew it was wrong, but didn't let myself dwell on it too long, so I just started copying them (not listening to my inner voice). While the first movie was loading onto my computer, my son Tristan walked in and saw what I was doing. Tristan was working at a movie theater at the time, and he asked me if I was copying the DVD. I couldn't believe what I did next... I fumbled and mumbled some sort of nonanswer. Then he said, "That's illegal, Mom." Punch me in the gut. I was so overwhelmed by my actions that I changed the subject and he left the room.

Good grief, what had I just done? I made more than one mistake. I compounded it, and it all stemmed from my embarrassment and not acting with integrity. Knowing the kind of person I want to be and the kind of parenting I want to model, I went out to talk with Tristan. I explained that I just erased the copy and would not copy disks that were not mine. I also told him I was sorry that I lied and that I was embarrassed. I further explained how proud I was that he asked me about it in the first place. Speaking truth to power is something I coach clients on all the time: can employees call out a boss for doing something wrong? There's always a risk. But in this case, I told Tristan I knew it was hard for a child to tell a parent that they were doing something wrong. I was proud that he did that. I want him to be someone who isn't afraid to inquire and call out questionable behavior. And for me, I practiced repairing trust with my son. I do not want him to think of me as someone without integrity. We all make mistakes, so we all can work to make things right.

Strengthen Relationships and Connectivity by Investing Time and Energy into Building Others Up, and Avoid Gossip, Which Erodes Self-Esteem and Group Connectivity

We have heard over and over again that nothing erodes trust faster than gossip. Spreading rumors and gossip tarnishes reputations and crushes people's self-esteem on the receiving end. And for those who spread rumors, the act itself tarnishes their reputations, too. These behaviors adversely affect psychological safety and trust levels in groups and are a recipe for a rapid downward spiral of your team. To keep healthy trust levels, stop the rumor mill. If hurtful or demeaning comments about someone reach you, stop them there and tell the people spreading the messages that you want no part in it and that these behaviors are hurtful. You are in the people-building business, so choose another path rather than listening to the latest gossip. People building is everyone's responsibility, not just those in leadership positions.

Be intentional and take time to strengthen people's relationships with each other. When you do this, you bolster connectivity. The stronger the connections are between people on your team, the more resilient your team is and the more able it is to handle challenges and setbacks.

As a consultant, when I work with groups, I am deliberate about introductory activities that build connectivity in the group right away. Even if the group has worked together for a long time, chances are they have not spent a lot of time getting to know each other personally. There is a dominant paradigm in Western culture that believes spending time on getting to know others is wasteful and not the real work. I unequivocally disagree with this thinking. Strengthening connectivity among people is real work. It has real payoffs when connectivity is strong, and there are clear inefficiencies when people don't get along.

Respect People's Unique Contributions, Honor Different Perspectives and Styles, and Be Inclusive and Welcoming

No two people are the same. You already know that. But respecting different contributions, perspectives, and styles takes skill and, at times, intentionality. Helping people feel welcome and included is everyone's job, not just the person leading the meeting or event. Have you ever walked into a meeting and no one recognized your presence? While this could be an introvert's dream, I am talking about a place where you felt unimportant or ignored. Building trust with others means scanning your environment to ensure people are plugged into the group. It means being mindful of helping people feel like they can bring their best selves to the group because the recognition of their unique contribution is important.

Indicators of Problems with Interpersonal Dynamics-Level Trust Behaviors

Interpersonal dynamics encompass the full range of human emotions and behaviors that can either help or erode trust. Indicators of problems include:

- People feeling ignored, shut down, dismissed, ridiculed, or disrespected
- Self-serving actions, often resulting in others being hurt or neglected
- Spreading rumors
- Dishonest and deceitful words and actions
- Insensitive, rude, judgmental, harassing, or bullying behavior
- Personality clashes and strong misalignment with culture
- Blaming, not acknowledging impact on others, not apologizing, not admitting mistakes or accepting responsibility

Trust Behaviors Framework Summary

These research-based behaviors build and strengthen trusting relationships. This framework will increase your ability to effectively lead people and can support you if trust erodes and you need to diagnose the source and determine strategies to repair it.

PURPOSE
Why the
Group Exists

- Determine purpose, direction, scope, priorities, and boundaries
- Align people, systems, and resources for success

ROLES
Who Does
What Function

- Establish clear roles, responsibilities, mutual expectations, and accountability
- Set people up for success, delegate well, and create support systems
- Honor agreements, commitments, and confidentiality

CORE
PROCESS
How Work
Gets Done

- Improve operations, relationships, and results; and be open to new ways of doing things
- Ensure consistency, reliability, and responsiveness
- Engage people, broaden decision-making, and ask for input

COMMUNICATION
How People
Share Information

- Listen openly without judgment or interruption, and tune in to the quiet voices
- Check in on assumptions, intentions, and mutual understanding
- Seek feedback, sound and current information, and new perspectives
- Share timely, relevant information; avoid surprises; and be transparent and truthful
- Foster curiosity and open-mindedness, and engage in healthy challenges to conventional thinking

INTERPERSONAL
DYNAMICS
How People
Interact

- Model high standards, integrity, and vulnerability
- Invest in the growth and development of others
- Acknowledge mistakes and your impact on others, and sincerely apologize in a timely manner
- Strengthen relationships and connectivity by investing time and energy into building others up, and avoid gossip, which erodes self-esteem and group connectivity
- Respect people's unique contributions, honor different perspectives and styles, and be inclusive and welcoming

Most Common Trust Violations: What Do the Numbers Mean?

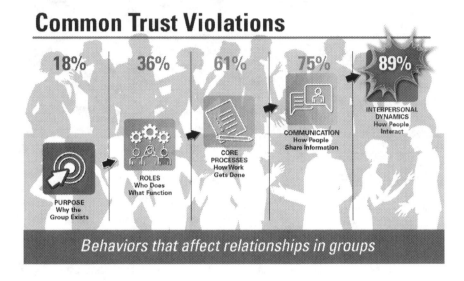

The percentages in the diagram stem from my doctoral research study on repairing trust in groups.[1] I interviewed people representing groups from every sector (public, private, nonprofit, education) and asked them to describe the violations of trust they experienced. In my original study, I placed the violations into eight categories. After further research and working with more clients since then, I synthesized the most common trust violations into five main categories: purpose, roles, core processes, communication, and interpersonal dynamics.

The percentages were derived by counting each time a participant noted a trust violation. For example, one participant group described three types of violations occurring for them: people were unclear about what to do (roles), they were not listening to each other (communication), and treating each other disrespectfully (interpersonal dynamics). Even if there were multiple interpersonal dynamic issues going on, I only counted once in each category if the violation description fit.

The percentages, by design, do not add up to 100 percent. Why? The percentages stem from the number of times participants in my trust repair study described violations of trust in that category; each participant could have multiple violations of trust. For example, of the trust violation experiences I analyzed in my study, 89 percent of the groups described issues relating to interpersonal dynamics. This means almost every group I interviewed described trust violations that included disrespectful behaviors, rude interactions, gossip, and other unhealthy dynamics. And, 75 percent of the groups also described communication issues stemming from the trust violations. When trust is violated, it can affect several areas.

Activities to Deepen Understanding

Reflection Questions

What makes you trustworthy?

Which of these trust behaviors are easy for you to use? Which are difficult? Why?

Take It Deeper

Think about a time when someone lost trust in *you* because you poorly executed some of these trust-building behaviors.
What happened?

What did you do about it? Did it work?

What was the impact on people and the work situation?

What was your intention behind your actions (or inactions)? Did your intention match your actions and get the desired outcome?

In hindsight, think about the trust behaviors in this chapter. What role did these trust behaviors play in your situation?

Short assignment #1
Discuss Trust Behaviors with a Group to Foster Learning

Review the trust behaviors framework in this chapter and ask fellow group members to describe times when they have

demonstrated these behaviors well. Any personal or professional story is fine to share. Take the time to engage in conversations about the behaviors. Be candid about what the group does well, why, and under what circumstances.

Then, inquire about the trust behaviors that within the group are not doing well. Discuss why.

Finally, move from describing what is not working well and focus attention on the future desirable state. What do we need to need to do to be more effective as a team? What will that look like? How can we support each other in this work?

Short Assignment #2
Individual Feedback on Your Trustworthiness

Gather feedback from three people who work closely with you on a regular basis. Give them the list of trust behaviors (outlined in this chapter) and have a conversation about which ones they experience from you that you do well, and which behaviors need improvement.

While it could be difficult, there is greater ability to strengthen relationships if you have these conversations in person. Although some people may slightly inflate the feedback, making it more positive, as a society, we need to get better at having conversations together.

Group Self-Assessment Tool

Below are the trust behaviors that support effective groups. Please select the number on the scale that best fits your opinion.

On a scale from 1 (low) to 5 (high), how well does this group (or person):

1. Determine purpose, direction, scope, priorities, and boundaries?
    (low)   1   2   3   4   5   (high)
2. Align people, systems, and resources for success?
    (low)   1   2   3   4   5   (high)
3. Establish clear roles, responsibilities, mutual expectations, and accountability?
    (low)   1   2   3   4   5   (high)
4. Set up people for success: delegate well and create support systems?
    (low)   1   2   3   4   5   (high)
5. Honor agreements, commitments, and confidentiality?
    (low)   1   2   3   4   5   (high)
6. Improve operations, relationships, and results, and be open to new ways of doing things?
    (low)   1   2   3   4   5   (high)
7. Ensure consistency, reliability, and responsiveness?
    (low)   1   2   3   4   5   (high)
8. Engage people, broaden decision-making, and ask for input?
    (low)   1   2   3   4   5   (high)
9. Listen openly without judgment or interruption, and tune in to the quiet voices?
    (low)   1   2   3   4   5   (high)
10. Check in on assumptions, intentions, and mutual understanding?
    (low)   1   2   3   4   5   (high)

11. Seek feedback, sound and current information, and new perspectives?
    (low)   1   2   3   4   5   (high)
12. Share timely, relevant information; avoid surprises; and be transparent and truthful?
    (low)   1   2   3   4   5   (high)
13. Foster curiosity and open-mindedness, and encourage healthy challenges to conventional thinking?
    (low)   1   2   3   4   5   (high)
14. Model high standards, integrity, and vulnerability?
    (low)   1   2   3   4   5   (high)
15. Invest in the growth and development of others?
    (low)   1   2   3   4   5   (high)
16. Acknowledge mistakes and impact on others, and sincerely apologize in a timely manner?
    (low)   1   2   3   4   5   (high)
17. Strengthen relationships and connectivity; invest time and energy into building others up; and avoid gossip, which erodes self-esteem and group connectivity?
    (low)   1   2   3   4   5   (high)
18. Respect people's unique contributions, honor differing perspectives and styles, and be inclusive and welcoming?
    (low)   1   2   3   4   5   (high)

This questionnaire can be broken out further to better evaluate each element. This can also make it less confusing regarding how to answer if you would answer one part of the question one way and another part of the question another way. For example, look at the first statement: Determine purpose, direction, scope, priorities, and boundaries. There are five sets of behaviors and actions within this statement. You might believe that the group you are in has solid purpose, but you are not clear about the priorities or direction.

To take this assessment to a more detailed level, break out the questions further. You can choose to keep the full statement:

1. Determine purpose, direction, scope, priorities, and boundaries?
   (low)   1   2   3   4   5   (high)

Or you can choose to break the statements out for further clarity:

1. Determine purpose?
   (low)   1   2   3   4   5   (high)
2. Determine direction?
   (low)   1   2   3   4   5   (high)
3. Determine scope?
   (low)   1   2   3   4   5   (high)
4. Determine priorities?
   (low)   1   2   3   4   5   (high)
5. Determine boundaries?
   (low)   1   2   3   4   5   (high)

Debrief Results With Your Team

You may ask team members to take the survey anonymously or discuss it openly in a meeting. The most important part is to discuss the results and identify a couple of areas that the team does well and appreciate it. Equally, figure out a few areas to work on improving. Do not overwhelm yourself with too many things to do.

CHAPTER 3
Trust Repair Model

Beyond being right and being wrong
there lies a field, I will meet you there.
—Rumi

Even with the best plans, good intentions, and hard work, sometimes things go sideways with other people, and you find yourself in a low-trust or broken trust situation. While every group experiences challenges and setbacks, there are times when you become stuck. The Trust Repair Model combines research and years of practice working with groups when they are most stuck and provides a process to explore and mend the situation. The model lays out four major phases of the trust repair process: reflect, understand, repair, and evolve. Within each phase, I suggest actions to support you working through activities to repair trust and strengthen relationships.

I have witnessed many groups working through this trust repair model with tremendous success. The research behind it is strong, and yet it is still evolving. There are things I am still learning about trust and how to repair it. In my experience, the single greatest indicator of a group repairing trust is your mindset. Do you want to repair trust and mend these relationships? My hope is that your answer is yes.

Trust Repair Model

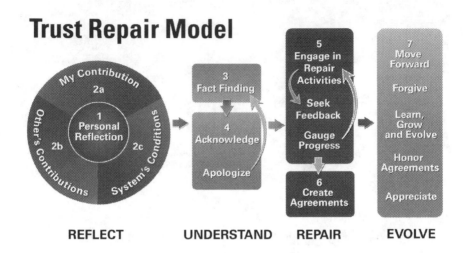

Phase Descriptions

The next few pages are a brief introduction into each phase of the Trust Repair Model. It is intended to be an overview so you can see how everything fits together. The next four chapters in the book are dedicated to deeply describing each phase and providing you with tools and examples so you can do the work.

Trigger Events

TRIGGER(S)

Sometimes trust within a group erodes over time because of a series of small things: missing soft deadlines, claiming emails were never received, or doing sloppy work, knowing that others in the group will fix it. After so many of these small events, just one more missed deadline can send someone's rage soaring, and then that person is blamed for overreacting. Other times, trust explodes over a single incident: missing an important event, not apologizing for embarrassing someone, breaking confidentiality, or doing sloppy work, causing angry customers.

Triggers are often personal and are fueled by our backgrounds, personality style, life experiences, and interactions over time with a person or group. Sometimes we are clear about what triggers affect us. Consider the analogy of taking luggage onto an airline. For some people, the circumstances that trigger their inner trust barometer can fit nicely into a rollaway bag and be placed in the compartment above the seats. Others have lots of bags and boxes, and they are stowed in the plane's cargo hold. Upon experiencing a trigger, you might find that the person has a lifetime of being marginalized and that one incident of being ignored at a meeting becomes a huge trust violation. You never know which passengers are traveling with only a carry-on and which have multiple suitcases in the cargo hold. We do not know each other's stories and personal barometers for deciding when an incident has elevated to a full trust violation. If a person says their trust is damaged, do not argue or trivialize their feelings, because it is not your experience. It is best at this stage to stay out of judgment and spend some time reflecting on what just happened, which is the first step in the Trust Repair Model.

Reflect Phase: Steps 1 and 2

As a first step, when someone feels triggered with emotions from trust violations, it is important to reflect on the experience. Interview the feelings by asking yourself: *Why am I feeling this way? Why did this situation bother me? Have I felt this way before? Is this about me or is it something that I will need to sort out with others?* Spending time deeply reflecting on your experience is the first thing you need to do.

The second step in the trust repair process is to consider everyone's parts in the trust violation scenario. People must first consider their own contribution to the situation, which is why reflection is the first phase in the model. Everyone plays a part in how the trust violations happened, whether they are conscious about it or not.

First, consider yourself. Then consider others on the team: what did they do to contribute to the situation? Normally, it is easy to think about what others did or did not do that triggered the trust violations. But then you need to consider the larger organization and any outside influences that may be impacting the group and trust situation. All these are at play in the reflect phase, which will be covered in depth in chapter 4.

Understand Phase: Steps 3 and 4

Fact-finding requires you find out what happened and collect sound and current information. Sound information is accurate and stems from reasonable viewpoints, studies, or real examples. Rumors, relying on your own interpretations or assumptions, or reacting to one thing is not sound. Think of a doctor only taking one measure of health, like your blood pressure, and calling you healthy. There are multiple indicators of health, and using only one measure is not sound. It is equally important to ensure you have current, recent, and timely information to support your thinking. People get stuck using old information and do not question if circumstances changed or if they are operating from old perspectives. For example, if a work colleague let you down a year ago by not following through on an assignment, do you still assume that if a team misses a deadline and that person is on the team, it is their fault? How do you know? You need to find out the facts regarding why the team missed the deadline by gathering sound and current information and staying out of assumption-land.

The key to fact-finding is to seek sound and current information from other people affected by the violations of trust. Be open and curious to what you hear, and stay away from judgment. Gandhi often talked about seeking the "third truth," which means you bring your truth about what happened, the other person brings their truth, and together you create the third truth. People are human and mess up or do not know they had an adverse impact on someone else. This fact-finding time is critical to putting together as many of the pieces of the puzzle as possible. Step 3 encompasses gathering sound and current facts from everyone involved.

Step 4 should occur naturally while you are fact-finding. Acknowledge your part and acknowledge if any pain occurred to the other person if you did something. Even if you didn't mean it, acknowledgment matters. Acknowledgment is critical to the trust repair process. If an apology is needed, make one sincerely and in a timely manner. Without proper acknowledgment or apologies, you can have all the facts and understand what happened but still not be able to move forward. Chapter 5 is dedicated to the understand phase. If this phase is done well, you may not need the rest of the model, because these steps significantly affect the psychological satisfaction of the people involved and increase the likelihood of repairing trust.

Repair Phase: Steps 5 and 6

Engaging in repair activities is the next phase of the Trust Repair Model. Depending on the situation, there are many ways to support teams as they work through repairing trust. The key is to have done good fact-finding in step 3 so you have a baseline of what to remedy here in step 5. Remember to seek feedback along the way to gauge progress toward your repair goals. In my research, I found that most teams take six to thirty-six months to work through repair activities. Be patient. Be intentional and know that you don't always nail it the first time out. Try several things and seek support from others to help you. I have found that the teams who engaged in several activities to repair trust were more likely to repair than the others who tried one or two things and gave up.

As you work through a variety of trust repair activities and make progress, you may need to create or modify agreements, which is step 6. Groups need structure and clear agreements about process, roles, and responsibilities, but they also need clarity about how they will communicate, make decisions, and work together. Agreements on the interpersonal side of trust repair are paramount. You may need to revise ground rules, update purpose statements, and generate rules of engagement, and you may even find value in outlining new procedures on how people will work through future challenges.

Evolve Phase: Step 7

Moving forward with trust repair means acceptance and forgiveness, but it also means honoring new agreements. Evolving is the fourth phase of the trust repair process. We must let people evolve past the moment when they let us down. We can't grow without challenges. And if people hold on to those moments, you may never be able to see the person in a new light. Moving forward does not mean forgetting what happened. It is a conscious choice to release yourself from being continually harmed by trust violations and to let others grow and learn from their mistakes. Chapter 7 explores forgiveness and resilience and will provide you with support to truly move forward.

Summary

The Trust Repair Model has four phases that each build upon the other: reflect, understand, repair, and evolve. Each phase has one or two steps within it that support the exploration and completion of activities that help repair trust in groups. While there is no guarantee that moving through the phases and steps will repair trust, there is evidence that some groups can successfully achieve higher levels of trust and stronger relationships by doing these activities. The next four chapters deeply describe the four phases and activities.

CHAPTER 4

Reflect

Humankind has not woven the web of life. We are but one thread within it. Whatever we do to the web, we do to ourselves. All things are bound together. All things connect.

—Chief Sealth, 1855

When something happens that shakes your trust in others, the first phase in the repair model invites you to stop and reflect on what happened. Many people are quick to search for external causes, focus on who is to blame, and stay there. That is natural. But what you really need to do first is silence your racing mind and reflect.

Step 1: Personal Reflection

1 Personal Reflection

Depending on what happened and how deeply you feel about the situation, you may need a cooling-off period. Those old adages that suggest things like "Don't send that email when you are angry" are passed along for good reason. When people have an emotional spike or reaction to something, it affects the chemistry in the brain. It evokes the fight-or-flight impulse (the amygdala, or "lizard brain"), and it makes people acutely sensitive to staying alive. However, when this happens, it prevents access to the full brain because it is focusing its attention on the vital parts of the body, which, sorry to say, is not your whole brain. When people say they have tunnel vision, the amygdala part of the brain has been activated. The result? The emotional reaction compromises (slows down) our ability to think clearly. Do yourself a favor and go for a walk or do something else relaxing to you. When the emotion level calms down, your cognitive level—your ability to think—raises back up, and you should have full use of your brain once again.

> *When you have an emotional spike, you do not have access to your full brain and muscles.*

In this very important reflection period, you need to explore what you are feeling and why it bothers you. You need to ask if this is *your* issue alone. Everyone has experiences from their past and present that shape their reactions to events. In my family, when someone was upset or angry, we would tell that person to relax. Instead of actually helping the person to relax, the suggestion itself became a trigger word that got our blood boiling. It was used over the years to placate us, imply that our feelings were not valid, or suggest that we should just "get over it." So, if someone else tells me to relax, it has an opposite effect! Sometimes hearing that word angers me. But do I need to repair trust with this person? Probably not. The reaction is my internal experience based on growing up in my family, and it is my issue.

Healthy repair of trust begins with you. It begins with your inner exploration of the impact of whatever the trigger was. So, interview the feelings that are coming up for you. It is important that you understand the background, history, and conditions that triggered these feelings for yourself. Ask questions like:

> *"People tend to talk about what others do. But we need to look at ourselves first."*
> —Brenda Jones

- What just happened?
- Why am I feeling this way?
- What bothers me the most about the situation?
- Has this happened to me before?
- Is this my issue alone?
- Do I need to work this out with someone else? My team? Who?

Step 2: Contributions

After you spend time personally reflecting, consider what is happening around you that contributed to the situation. What is happening with you, and others, and with the larger group that is influencing the situation? Step 2 of the Trust Repair Model is still in the Reflect phase, and it broadens your thinking beyond how the trust violation impacted you and what contributed to it happening in the first place. There are three questions in step 2 to think about:

- What did you contribute to the situation?
- What did others contribute?
- What conditions were present in the system that also influenced the situation?

These are systems thinking questions, and they are a foundational element in this trust repair model.

Systems Thinking

I believe that understanding systems thinking is essential for repairing trust with others. *A system is a set of interrelated, interdependent, and connected parts that form a complex whole. It contains both tangible parts (people, jobs, equipment) and intangible parts (procedures, rules, policies, communication patterns, values and beliefs, roles people play).[1]*

> "The quality and productivity of any group is directly proportional to quality of the connectedness within that system."
>
> —Michael Broom and Edie Seashore

That is why when something happens in a group that affects trust, everyone is contributing to it either by direct action or inaction because you are all part of the group system. For example, two work colleagues get into a heated argument at a staff meeting that causes trust to erode in the group. It is typically not just about the two people. You are there as a part of the group, and even if you did nothing during the exchange, you have been affected by it and you affected the situation, too. This also means that you have the choice to do something about it.

Individual Complexity

The complexity of trust begins at birth with personal innate attributes, and it evolves over time as people have experiences and mature. Things that contribute to the uniqueness of each person include:

- Personality style
- Emotional intelligence
- Core values
- Maturity level
- Race/ethnicity
- Age
- Gender identity
- Sexual identity
- Life experiences

- Cultural influences
- Family of origin
- Motivation
- Openness
- Education
- Connectedness with others
- Knowledge, skills, and abilities

All these areas, and others that are not described here, have the potential to affect relationships, behaviors, decisions, and reactions from the individual. People have different reactions to events given the circumstances and the complexity of their unique self.

For example, my father was a mechanical engineer, an introverted thinker, and a sensitive person. While I was in high school, he tried to help me with algebra. If I did not understand something, I would ask him to repeat his explanation. Sometimes the concepts just did not sink in, so I kept asking him to repeat the points. After several iterations of this, he took offense and got a little edgy with me. I felt hurt. He felt hurt. Why? His personality style was one that if people questioned him, he saw it as they were questioning his competency. However, for me, asking questions is how I learn. Even with his best explanations, sometimes it took a while for concepts to sink in. If we didn't have

> "If you judge people, you have no time to love them."
> —Mother Theresa

such an investment in our relationship as father and daughter and he was just a neighbor helping me, I probably would have never asked for help again, and he may have written me off too.

Remember, you do not fully know another person's life story, even those who are close to you. You do not know their trust experiences over time and everything else that makes up that beautifully unique individual. You did not know that the word *relax* has an opposite reaction for me, but now you do. You may not know if you trigger an experience or reaction in someone else by using certain words, gestures, and approaches that only that person is sensitive to. What people experience is the reaction and they interpret it through their own filters. In the Reflect phase, you must consider how these various attributes may be affecting the situation. And certainly, do not judge the reaction of others in this phase. Everyone has a different set of experiences that shapes them. Be curious and open, rather than judgmental.

Social and emotional intelligence strategies can support you in becoming more aware of your needs and building the capacity to tune in to others and assess situations. Richard Boyatzis and Daniel Goleman have developed an instrument that I found useful over the years in helping people learn and gauge social and emotional intelligence.[2] Are you aware of and can you manage your emotions and behaviors given different circumstances? That is emotional and social intelligence. Understanding this fosters your ability to assess situations and strengthen relationships, which are some of the key ingredients to repairing trust with others.

Bottom line: be mindful and pay attention to the impact you are having on others and the impact they have on you. Know your story and interview any feelings that arise when you are triggered by some event or behavior. The more conscious you are, the more you can manage your reaction and keep the emotional spikes down. Consider the other people's stories and their unique attributes that are also at play in the situation. Take the time to reflect on individual complexity without judgment.

Group Complexity

A group, made up of unique and complex individuals, can bring multiple combinations of the attributes as well. They become part of the group's genetic code. As the group has shared experiences, these experiences create and shape its culture and the way it operates. Groups are also influenced by the leaders, other groups, and the larger organization. A group's ability to repair trust is influenced by many things, such as:

- Culture
- Shared experiences
- Core work
- Training and learning together
- Who is on the team
- Who the leader is
- How well they know each other
- Larger organizational influences on the team
- Structure, purpose, mission, charter, roles, responsibilities, policies, and rules

Kurt Lewin, a social psychologist and one of the foundational thinkers in the field of sociology and organization development, studied groups and how people behave in social situations. He suggested that behavior is a function where people interact with their environment:[3]

$$B = f(P,E)$$

B = Behavior demonstrated
f = function
P = People (personality style, personal characteristics, etc.)
E = Environment (setting, culture of the group, type of group, influences)

For example, even though I am the same person and believe I bring my authentic self to each engagement, I make different choices about my behaviors depending on the group environment. I may use different words, tone, and stories to communicate with old college friends than I would use at work with business colleagues. The choices I make about my behavior are a function of my unique self in different environments.

This equation is important to understanding how to repair trust in groups because it is a reminder that the environment and the people influence behaviors. If a group's culture and the way people interact within the group are not going so well, consider what is happening in the environment of that group along with the unique styles of each person. There will be many things to consider that may shed light on the situation.

For example, is it okay to question authority in your group? Maybe in your current group it is okay to check in, question assumptions, and offer new possible ways of doing the work, regardless of any rank in the room. But, if you go to another group and start questioning the leader, what if you find the group members all look at you as if you were from another planet? You have not changed, but the environment is different and therefore the behaviors are different, too. This new group must have some shared experiences whereby the members are reinforcing cultural expectations about acceptable behaviors; clearly, questioning authority is taboo.

The complexity of groups is fascinating and examining people's behaviors provides meaningful clues for strengthening and repairing trust.

Organizational and Global Complexity

Groups are also affected by larger organizations and the local and global communities in which they reside. Trust is influenced by things like the global economy because it affects the number of customers purchasing services and goods from an organization. Those organizations, responding to customer demand, may place more pressure on their internal groups to satisfy those customers, and therefore meeting performance levels becomes a priority. Those priorities trickle down to pressure on individual supervisors and workers. Pressure from outside the group can cause stress and tension, which can contribute to poor interpersonal dynamics. See the interconnectivity of systems thinking? Here are some larger system influences that can affect your work:

- Economy
- Competition
- Community
- Access to talent
- Access to resources
- Changes in regulations (e.g., local, national, international)
- Customer and stakeholder expectations
- Parent organization
- Uncommon events (e.g., natural disasters, political uncertainty)

Some of my trust study participants described challenges and influences from their larger systems. Team members can get snarky with each other when they are under pressure from the parent organization. Trust is more fragile during these stressful times. Keep in mind that your team members pay attention to the financial picture, customer sentiment, performance pressures, and other influences that affect your organization. These, in turn, affect trust behaviors within groups.

It Is Your Choice

The Reflect phase is about *you*. Inviting you to get centered and think about what happened and providing you an opportunity to make a deliberate choice about if, when, and how to move forward with repairing trust. You choose to move forward or not with trust repair strategies after thinking about all that may have contributed to the situation. It may feel like it is a stretch for your skills or one that takes courage to face. You could ignore it, let it go, or pretend it did not bother you as much.

Harvard Business Review reported that managing people is a time-consuming task. Money is wasted each day on areas like unproductive conflict and problems that are ignored for fear of conflict.[4] Fear is one of the biggest hurdles to overcome for human beings, and it has been known to emotionally paralyze people. Ignoring the problem only makes things worse. You have a choice to face your fears or sit in misery.

> *Money is wasted each day on areas like unproductive conflict and problems that are ignored for fear of conflict.*

There is a little-known phenomenon called the Zeigarnik effect that states that people remember uncompleted or interrupted tasks better than completed tasks.[5] As part of her doctoral thesis, she studied how incomplete tasks cause tension in our mind. What does this mean for trust? We replay in our minds moments when we experienced trust violations. When this happens, it takes energy, time, and erodes our ability to focus on other things if we keep playing the scenario over in our heads. If this is happening to you, it is a signal that you need to work through the issues. Be intentional and make a choice to work on repairing trust; use the model or help yourself put it to rest. Chapter 9 offers you some strategies on moving forward.

Trust Repair Study: Evidence of the Reflect Phase

I am curious about what helps some groups succeed in repairing trust versus those who do not succeed, so for my doctoral research, I studied it. To be a part of the study, a group must have experienced a violation or multiple violations of trust, tried to repair it, and either claimed they repaired trust or they did not. The participants were predominantly in the United States and Canada, and one had business operations in several Latin American countries. Every sector was represented in the study: private sector groups from large multinational organizations to medium-sized and small businesses; nonprofit sector; higher education, including large research universities, community colleges, and private educational institutions; and public-sector organizations ranging from local to state to federal government and groups of elected officials.

Out of the groups that claimed they were successful in repairing trust, 73 percent reported that they had people reflecting about the trust violations and thought about what to do to repair it. Some took time to ensure they fully understood where things were before proceeding or let themselves heal if the violation affected them personally, and then considered next steps. Here are some quotes representing some of the study participants' use of reflection in their trust repair process:

> Sujul: I came home and started thinking about what was really going on.

> Joan: We thought about it. We knew that we were in the wrong.

> Steve: We espouse being a learning organization, and yet we have blown it. What is up with that? We had to stop and think. What do we need to learn about ourselves?

> Abigail: So all these things were running through my mind as I processed this...because I am a processer. I needed to think about these things. Eventually, I decided, "Well, I am going to take a chance and go and talk to this person."

Only 15 percent of the groups that were not successful in repairing trust spent any time reflecting about the situation first before any action. However, in hindsight, most of the people in my study, whether their group repaired trust or not, reported wishing they had built in more time to reflect about the trust violations and situation.

> Rosa: I felt like I didn't dedicate enough time to the board. I did not dedicate enough time thinking about it, and I was impatient.

> Fred: I think we had normal pressures of getting work done on time. None of us really wanted to go think about it and go deep because it was deeper than we would be able to resolve quickly.

Summary

The first phase of the Trust Repair Model is Reflect, and it has two steps. The first step is to personally reflect on the situation and any triggers you experienced that affect trust and relationships. Reflect on your feelings, thoughts, and what is at stake for you. The second step is to reflect on what you contributed to the situation, what others contributed, and what is happening in the larger system that is influencing people and work.

Taking time to reflect is an important function of repairing trust in groups. As you give yourself this gift of time, you will be determining if you need to move forward with trust repair activities or if the situation rests with you alone. Making a deliberate choice frees you from being stuck and allows you to move into the Understand phase of the model.

Further Your Learning and Use of the Model

I offer two sets of practical tools to further your learning.

- Activities to deepen understanding: At the end of this chapter you will find individual reflection questions and short assignments designed to deepen your understanding of the chapter content.
- Reflect tools: In chapter 10 I have provided three tools with descriptions of how to use them with individuals or in groups. Most tools are coupled with a real example of using the tool with a group or individual to aid in your learning

and understanding of how to use and adapt the tool to your trust situation. The intention is to give you immediate tools to support working with repairing trust in your group.

- Reflection Questions
- Trust Assessment
- Choice Matrix

Activities to Deepen Understanding

Reflection Questions

Think of a time when you experienced something that shook your trust in others. How did you react? What did you think and feel?

Now, write the biography of these feelings. Where did they come from? What beliefs underscore them? Interview each feeling and get clear about its story.

Short Assignment #1: Personal Triggers and Strategies

TRIGGER(S)

For every action, there is a reaction. The more you understand what bothers, upsets, embarrasses, or angers you, the better you'll be at managing it. That doesn't mean you'll not feel those things. You will just be in a better place to not let your emotions spike too long.

Do your own assessment of what triggers you. Make a list. Think about when you feel most triggered: is it a certain kind of person, behavior, or experience?

Then, think about what strategies have helped you before when you are emotionally triggered. What are strategies you use to calm down?

CHAPTER 5

Understand

There is nothing that exists that has only one side. Even a piece of paper, thin as it is, has two sides

—Terry Goodkind

The Understand phase of the Trust Repair Model centers on getting clear about what happened. This phase entails listening with an open mind to the facts, bearing the emotions, and learning about the impact the situation had on the people involved. This phase should not be rushed. If you hurry through learning about what happened, you may miss important clues that people share about what they need to move forward. You need to remain curious, listen to other perspectives, and keep your ego in check. You will need to acknowledge and apologize for your part, whether you intended it or not; you will learn that you had an impact on the situation and other people. In this Understand phase, other people will also hear from you and need to acknowledge the impact their actions had on you. To move forward, all people involved will need to offer apologies sincerely and in a timely manner if they become necessary. Not every action and perceived violation of trust needs an apology, but every action needs your understanding and acknowledgment of its impact.

If you do this phase well, you may not need the rest of the Trust Repair Model. Why? Because most of the time, people crave feeling heard and acknowledged that they were hurt by others and want an appropriate apology. When they get that, they may not need repair activities in the next phase because the emotional burden has been lifted.

Step 3: Fact-Finding

Give each person an uninterrupted opportunity to speak their truth. Listen to their description of the chronology of events. While listening, tune in to the emotional impact in their story. Be curious: Why did the situation hurt them? What were their intentions behind any of their actions or inaction? Did their intentions match the impact you (and others) experienced? Stay involved in fact-finding and consider it an opportunity to surface, explore, and make sense of what happened for each person affected by the violation of trust in the group.

While fact-finding, you can expect to hear people explain away their own mistakes or violations of trust due to external reasons or some other noble purpose. At the same time, people tend to hold others accountable for the perceived injustices or hurt they caused and want those remedied. People do this because they consider their own motives to be honorable or principled. Without judgment or arguing with them, in this early part of listening, simply acknowledge that you are hearing them. *Acknowledgment does not mean you agree with them*; it is about letting the person know you are listening and that you understand them. You might ask clarifying questions to further your understanding. In return, ask that they give you the same courtesy and nonjudgment as you explain your story of what

> *You are making a big mistake if you think that you already know the facts and do not need to listen to the other people explain their story.*

happened, your intentions, and the impact the situation has had on you. It is a powerful experience for people to actually hear what the intentions are behind someone's actions because initially there are a lot of assumptions made and this leads to misunderstandings and violations of trust.

You are making a big mistake if you think that you already know the facts and do not need to listen to the other people explain their story. I sometimes hear, "I know what she meant." I question right back: "*How* do you know?" People make assumptions and believe their own thinking without getting sound and current information. How recent is the information you are working with to determine the facts? As a consultant, I sometimes hear claims like "All the employees are concerned about *X*." *All* is a strong claim. I am curious whether there is data to support this claim. It makes me wonder: how many employees actually said they were concerned about *X*? Sometimes people react to just a couple of people saying something and believe it must be true for everyone. Two experiences typically do not constitute sound data and information. You must combat missing sound and current information by asking people for their input and gathering current information, because the data continually changes.

> *"We dance around a ring and suppose, while the truth sits in the middle and knows."*
> —Robert Frost

Without sound and current information, people tend to fabricate their own data to support their thinking. What is preventing people from having the conversations they need together to generate sound and current information? Typically, it is fear. Fear of facing people, whom you believe wronged you, to get the facts. There is also fear of potentially learning that your judgment or impressions are wrong or misguided. Instead of facing these fears, people sit in misery, make up facts, or believe only information that supports their thinking. They tell themselves

> *We judge ourselves by our intent...yet, we judge others by their impact.*

stories about how the other folks are really rotten and wanted to hurt them, rather than explore the situation with them in person. It is a story that keeps them in a righteous place in their mind and makes the other person out to be the villain. The result of all of this is a lot of finger pointing and people staying stuck living in "assumption land."

Some work environments punish people for being wrong. This causes a whole set of unhealthy behaviors. People may fear that admitting mistakes, taking responsibility, or being associated with the failures will result in public ridicule, diminished opportunities, or other painful ramifications. Innovation and creativity thrive in places where people feel free to make and learn from mistakes, because it is a source of growth. Make it safe for yourself and others to learn from mistakes, seriously consider alternative viewpoints, and be open to new information.

Another reason why people need to gather sound and current information is that human memory and recall work nothing like computers. There are conflicting studies about fear and recall of memory. Some studies say people can remember every vivid detail, and other studies showed people inflated or lost facts over time. One study looked at people's memories and likened it to what they called flash bulb memories. Phelps Lab is in New York City, and their employees experienced the September 11, 2001, terrorist attacks. They conducted a large detailed survey at these specific time periods: a few weeks after the attacks, one year, two years, and ten years. The survey asked the same questions at each interval to the same people and while "People were very confident that their details were correct," the data showed that their recollections changed over time. This study supports the notion that emotion focuses your attention on a few details at the expense of the others.[1] It also suggests that facts can change in people's minds over time even though they are adamant that they know precisely what happened. The message here is that you can believe wholeheartedly that you have all the facts and understand them, but you can still be wrong. You must go through the fact-finding stage and be open to exploring the situation.

Do you like being wrong? Most people hate it. The discomfort of being wrong has a lot to do with ego management and identity. Egos and people's core beliefs get in the way of letting in real facts and new information. Talk to yourself in a way that takes the pressure off being right so you can be open to learning in this Understand phase. I use an excellent TED Talk by Kathryn Schulz titled "On Being Wrong" (filmed March 2011) quite often to get people thinking about the importance of being open to the possibility of being wrong. When we do, a whole new world opens.

One of the best ways to conduct fact-finding in a supportive way is to use a form of mediation. Good mediation has clear ground rules: listen, do not interrupt, and each person gets to completely share their story. Then the next person gets to tell their story. While people are talking, there are no gestures, words, or other nonverbal messages (e.g., eye rolling; heavy sighs) that may be used to express disapproval or disrespect. Mediation is an excellent way to help people feel heard. You can use the principles of mediation without having a neutral third party there to serve as the mediator. However, depending on the intensity of the situation, having a skilled person to support this conversation can relieve tension and help people talk. This is a great time for individuals or the group to use previous training models or tools they have learned in communication and conflict management to help them listen and identify issues.

Here are some examples from my study of participants whose groups successfully repaired trust. These quotes reflect the points raised in this fact-finding stage:

> Tamarah: We talked about things: "How what you said really hurt me and this is why; and, what in the world did I do to you to make you respond this way?" We each got our air time.

> Abigail: So we had the crucial conversation (relating to the book and training the group took together). She said that she didn't mean to breach

confidentiality and it just slipped out and she didn't realize that it would cause such problems.

Madi: We knew the breach of trust had happened by one member of the team. We didn't know exactly who, though. We talked about it at that meeting and said this person needs to come forward. But no one did. So, the next meeting we wouldn't go on with the content until we found out. Then the lady finally admitted she broke trust with the group. So, we asked her, "Should you leave? How can we count on you to fulfill your obligations? Why did you do this?"

Only 15 percent of participants who reported that their group did not repair the violation of trust made attempts to understand what the issues were and gather facts. Participants reported that people who were involved just did not want to go deep into the issues; they seemed to be unwilling to learn from the other side or just did not care. Here is one example to illustrate this point:

Marcel: My attempt was to bring people together and say, "Listen, we have a problem. And we are going to talk about it and we are going to get feelings about one another out on the table so we can deal with it and understand the different points of view." But, I think at that point the group was too far gone in having come to their conclusions about one another.

Step 4: Acknowledge and Apologize

Step 4 in the Trust Repair Model has two parts: acknowledge and apologize as necessary. This is a symbiotic relationship with fact-finding that makes up the essence of the Understand phase. As you learn what happened from each person affected, you immediately have an opportunity to acknowledge your part, clear up any misunderstanding, own your mistakes, and apologize. If you did not mean to harm anyone, but someone was hurt by your action or inaction, then at a minimum you need to acknowledge that pain occurred for that person or group, even though it was not your intent. In helping people move for-

> Without acknowledgment, even if you think you have remedied the problems, people stay psychologically and emotionally stuck.

ward, acknowledgment is more important than coming up with the right answer or having the right process whereby you made the decision. Unwillingness to acknowledge your part makes others feel insignificant or like they do not matter. Without acknowledgment, even if you think you have remedied the problems, people stay psychologically and emotionally stuck.

One year, I taught full time at a university and had an extraordinary amount of work designing semester-long classes for the first time and setting up a system to manage student work. In December of that year, an old military friend of my husband's reached out to me and asked if I could review his son Brent's résumé and coach him on other parts of the job search process. His son was a student at the university but was in another degree program. I agreed, and Brent sent me his résumé within a few days of my reply.

The email with his résumé sat in my inbox for four months. I was overcommitted and exhausted, trying to keep up with my obligations, while that email sat in my inbox eating at me. Every time I looked at the email, I constructed in my head some excuses that I could tell Brent. "I'm sorry, but my reply back to you was stuck in my draft folder and I didn't realize it." Or, the classic weasel response that I lost it or never received it. I was embarrassed about how long it sat untouched and very much wanted to escape the berating of myself for failing to respond in a timely manner. But lying and making up excuses lacked integrity, and that did not align with my core values.

In March, four months after he first contacted me, I emailed Brent back. I took full responsibility and ownership for not responding back in a timely manner and I apologized. I simply told him the truth, owned my failure, and offered to make it right by reviewing his résumé and meeting with him if he still wanted it. It was hard at first to admit my failure, but once I hit Send on that email, I felt a great sense of relief. Within the week, Brent and I met and we worked on his résumé. I acknowledged that my delay in responding put a crunch on his summer internship application process and sincerely apologized, and he accepted it.

Meaningful acknowledgment and apologies mean keeping your ego in check. I could have easily relied upon my position as a faculty member and expressed how busy I was so I could evade my embarrassment by waving my status as a busy faculty member, but that would have only fed my ego and still not have solved the problem that I broke a commitment and let someone down. Successful repair of trust and strengthening of relationships comes with understanding that you have an impact on others, so you need to acknowledge it.

In my study, out of all the groups that reported repairing trust, 67 percent used some sort of acknowledgment; they acknowledged a personal contribution to the situation, that someone was hurt, or that work was affected.

> Madi: She knew it had an impact on us and felt bad about it. She wanted to use this as a learning experience and hoped to be allowed to stay in the group.

> Joan: I think more important than the apology was that we started to understand the pressures of their world. I just knew that I lost face, and I essentially learned more about her and what motivates her and what she likes and how she likes to work. And I just worked the ways that she likes people to work with her. Eventually we got to having a good relationship and she started to listen to me and I

told her about our side. This helped to clear up the misunderstanding.

Interestingly, out of the participants who claimed their group did not repair trust, only 8 percent stated there was any sort of acknowledgment from the people involved in the violation. That means 92 percent did not acknowledge anything. No wonder these groups failed at trying to repair trust. There is a strong connection between acknowledgment and trust repair. Participants described actions such as taking no ownership for any part in the violation, blaming everyone else for the problems, dismissing their part in contributing anything to the situation, and disregarding any hurt that anyone else experienced. Here are several examples:

> Tony: It's important to understand some character-istics of Latin American people and culture. When I went on business there, I learned the whole reason why they didn't send [the survey data]. It wasn't given any importance. Sometimes it would take a lot for them to gather the information that the parent com-pany wanted. When they didn't hear anything back from the corporation, they thought, why bother?

> Hector: There was a reaction like "Don't blame us. Blame the board for not paying attention. Blame the other people." So, I said, "I'm not blaming you, but you are here, and it doesn't matter who is at fault—it is our responsibility every day to fix it." That mes-sage did not sit well with them.

> James: He was coming in late, missing meetings, not sharing information. There were a lot of activities that were impacting the team. He said that it was my choice to take him off the rotation, so any lost trust was my fault.

Lauren: There was no ownership. Outward blame only.

Frances: The one thing that stuck out in my mind is this rock. She had a series of rocks on her table with words on them. After I had expressed my concerns to her, she asked me to pick a rock and talk about it. The one I picked said *integrity*. She did not respond; she just looked at me. No validation, no acknowledgment. It's like she didn't hear a word I said or appeared to have cared at all.

Apologies

Good fact-finding means listening openly, without judgment, in an attempt to get everything out in the open. As you listen to each other, it becomes an opportunity to acknowledge your part and allow others to acknowledge their part. If the situation warrants it, a sincere apology completes the Understand phase.

One of my favorite researchers in the field of trust and repair is Roy Lewicki from The Ohio State University. I was honored to have him serve as my external reader on my doctoral research committee. In 2016, Lewicki partnered with fellow researchers Beth Polin and Robert Lount and studied apologies.[2] They found six elements that people need in an apology for it to matter:

1. An expression of regret for the offense; saying "I'm sorry"
2. An explanation of why the offense occurred
3. An acknowledgment of responsibility for causing the offense
4. A declaration of "repentance" that the violator will not repeat the offense
5. An offer to repair whatever damage may have been caused by the offense
6. A request for forgiveness for having committed the offense

In their research, they found that all six of these apology elements were not equal. Three stood out as more substantial: acknowledgment, declaring that the violator will not repeat the offense, and offering to repair whatever damage was done.

As I read their work, I thought about a model I learned in a mediation course, specifically the Satisfaction Triangle by Christopher Moore. To get a durable resolution, a decision that will stick, you need three things: substantive, procedural, and psychological satisfaction.[3]

Satisfaction Triangle

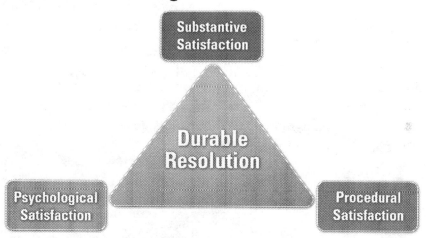

© C. Moore, The Mediation Process: Practical Strategies for Resolving Conflict, 4th ed., 2014. Used with permission of John Wiley and Sons, Inc., San Francisco, California.

- Substantive satisfaction means the decision or resolution focused on the right things, the root causes, and the true issues. It is focusing on the "right stuff."
- Procedural satisfaction encompasses the process that was set up to engage in the discussion and decisions: Was it fair? Did everyone have a chance to speak? Were the steps clearly laid out? Was all the evidence considered? This means having the "right steps" in the process.

- Psychological satisfaction means the people felt respected, listened to, and treated well in the process. This means that it "feels right" to the people involved.

For example, you can have a fair process set up and talk about the right things, but if people do not feel respected or heard, the psychological satisfaction component has not been met. If any of the three satisfaction components are not met, then the likelihood of the resolution or decision sticking greatly diminishes.

How does the Satisfaction Triangle relate to apologies and the repair of trust? By combining Lewicki, Polin, and Lount's research findings with Moore's Satisfaction Triangle model, you can see that if people only use the less preferred elements of an apology—saying "I'm sorry," offering an explanation of why it happened, and asking for forgiveness—it may not be enough to get a meaningful apology and may not stick. Placing these three less-preferred elements on the Satisfaction Triangle below, I show the lines further away from the center of the pyramid: the durable resolution, or the core of a lasting and meaningful apology.

Weak Apology
Low likelihood of a meaningful and durable apology

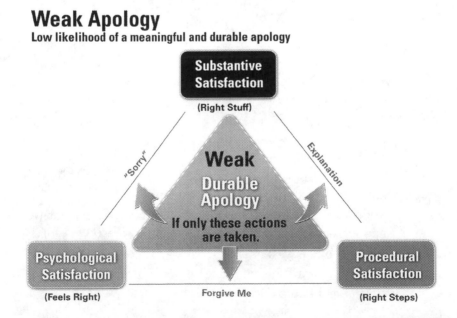

I see this in action with groups I consult with. After discussing the situation and determining the causes, if a person says "Sorry" with insincerity in their voice, explain why they did something, and ask for forgiveness, the apology typically fails. People know when there is an insincere apology. It is like they have a truth meter that gauges the sincerity level. The right apologetic words come out, but if the meaning and sincerity do not match, it does not stick. Offering reasons why something happened can help, but it will matter where blame and responsibility land. When explanations fall short, it is because the person apologizing may be explaining away the situation without understanding the impact it had on others. Even though people want to know what happened, this is still a less preferred apology element than understanding the impact, acknowledgment, offering to repair the wrong, and declaring that it will not happen again.

Strong Apology
High likelihood of a meaningful and durable apology

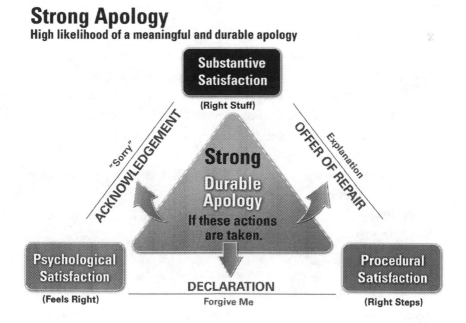

Lewicki, Polin, and Lount found that out of the six actions that help with meaningful apologies, the three that were most substantial were acknowledgment, a declaration that they will not repeat the offense, and offering to repair whatever they can to make things right again. I believe their research fits well with psychological, procedural, and substantive satisfaction, which is why these three preferred elements in an apology are closer to the durable resolution: the acceptance of the apology itself.

True acknowledgment supports both psychological and substantive satisfaction. A person admits that they had an impact on someone else or the system, and they name it. A declaration to not do it again also supports psychological satisfaction and becomes a necessary step in the process to repair. And finally, the offer to repair the wrong supports the procedural and substantive satisfaction bands because it deepens the intensity to right the wrongs.

In another study on apologies, Lewicki and Edward Tomlinson found that there are other conditions under which apologies are more likely to be effective:[4]

- Timely: when it is offered soon after the violation of trust
- Sincerity: when it is offered in a sincere emotional tone
- Responsibility: when the apologizer takes personal responsibility for creating the trust violation, rather than trying to blame it on some external event or source/person
- Isolated event: when the event that caused the breakdown was an isolated event rather than a repeat occurrence
- No harm: when the trust violation did not have severe consequences
- Integrity: when the event was not caused by some deceptive action on the part of the violator

In my study on repairing trust in groups, the participants who reported that their group repaired trust believed apologies strengthened their repair outcomes. The apologies were sincere and given within a close time frame after the violations of trust occurred. Here are some apologies from the groups that repaired trust:

Abigail: She apologized and said, "I am so sorry!" That was such a relief, and it started our journey to fixing the issues.

Hector: I apologized to angry callers and donors. I worked to get back to them with the information and results they wanted.

Peter: I apologized to this man. He shouldn't have been blamed for the situation.

Not surprisingly, in my study there were zero apologies from the groups that did not repair trust. Whenever I ask audiences to guess this number, they are correct right away. To successfully repair trust in groups, you must care enough to listen to each story, acknowledge your part, and apologize for any impact. I did not find anyone who repaired trust without an effective apology.

> *Not surprisingly,...there were zero apologies from the groups that did not repair trust.*

In addition, saying "I'm sorry you were offended by my actions" is not an apology. You are simply blaming the other person for the situation that resulted in broken trust. Instead, say "I'm sorry my actions offended you." You could strengthen the statement by including all the elements of successful apologies: "I'm sorry my actions offended you and negatively affected you meeting your deadline. Please know that I have made adjustments to my procedures, so I should have my part for the report ready on time in the future. Is there anything else that I can do to fix my mistake now?"

Summary

The second phase of the Trust Repair Model is Understand, and it has two symbiotic steps. Fact-finding is the third step of the repair model and asks you to find out all you can about what happened. You already know what happened from your perspective, but this step is specifically about finding out about what other people experienced and what they intended. Many misunderstandings get cleared up when you take the appropriate amount of time to explore everyone's perspectives.

The fourth step in the model underscores the importance of acknowledging the impact you had on others, whether it was intentional or not. Acknowledgment and an appropriate apology do more to repair relationships and meet the psychological needs of people than anything else.

If you listen without judgment, acknowledge your part, and apologize, you may not need the rest of the Trust Repair Model, because these actions help people feel understood and strengthen relationships.

Further Your Learning and Use of the Model

I offer two sets of practical tools to further your learning:

- Activities to deepen understanding: At the end of this chapter you will find individual reflection questions and short assignments designed to deepen your understanding of the chapter content.
- Understand tools: In chapter 10 I have provided some tools with descriptions of how to use them with individuals or in groups. Most tools are coupled with a real example of using the tool with a group or individual to aid in your learning and understanding of how to use and adapt the tool to your trust situation. The intention is to give you immediate tools to support working with repairing trust in your group.
  - Ladder of Inference
  - Mediation
  - Video and Discussion: "On Being Wrong"

Activities to Deepen Understanding

Reflection Questions

First, reflect on the statement: "We judge ourselves by our intent, yet we judge others by their impact."

Think about the times when you have felt misunderstood or misjudged.

What was that like?

What did you experience?

Did you try to discuss it with the other person? What happened?

Think about a time when you misunderstood or misjudged another person because of the impact they had on you, only to learn later about their true intention.

How did their actions impact you?

What were your original perceptions or judgments about that person?

When you found out their original intentions, how did that change your thinking?

What strategies can you use to get better at discerning someone's intent versus reacting to the impact you experience?

Team Discussion: Sound and Current Information

Gather your team and plan a forty-five- to sixty-minute conversation about sound and current information. Begin with a story of yours to illustrate the concept.

For example, I might share about a time when I was on a team and we believed we could not change a particular step in the process because it was written into laws. We were adamant about it and would not let the question surface in our conversations because it was pointless. We found out later, when someone actually read the law, that we had the ability to change the step we needed to. We wasted a lot of time and squashed innovative ideas because we used old information.

Ask your team to begin with some short answers:
What do we mean by sound data and information? What do we mean by current data and information?

How do we know if we are operating with sound and current information?

How can we make it safe for everyone here to question our data and information without feeling shut down? Remember, data changes all the time, so we must be ready and willing to question our thinking, our data, and the information we are using to make decisions.

What specific ideas or strategies do you suggest our team embrace to strengthen our ability to ask for and use sound and current information?

CHAPTER 6
Repair

Unless someone like you cares a whole awful lot, nothing is going to get better. It's not.

—Dr. Seuss, *The Lorax*

When groups reach the Repair phase of the Trust Repair Model, they have identified the core issues that contributed to the violations of trust that they experienced. Sometimes, the first two phases are all that are needed to repair trust because it helps people clear up misunderstandings, clarify intent, express acknowledgment of any impact, and apologize. When this happens, some people can move forward working together.

Sometimes during the Understand phase, people identify areas that need to improve or more time may be needed to work through the issues. This is the creative response to those identified needs. The Repair phase has the next two steps in the Trust Repair model: engage in repair activities in a way that gauges progress on whether you are improving the situation, and create any new agreements based on the repair activity outcomes that the group needs to move forward.

Step 5: Engage in Repair Activities

The Repair phase uses action research principles to help groups solve their own problems and move forward. Action research engages people who are affected by a problem in a reflective process that has four parts: assess the situation to get a baseline, design activities to improve the situation, engage in those activities, and seek feedback to gauge whether they improved.[1] The process is cyclical and repeated several times until the group reaches a point where they believe they have addressed the core problem and made meaningful progress. The process is finished when they document the progress, summarize any best practices that emerged, and create agreements.

Another finding from Google's mega study on the characteristics of high-performance teams suggests that people who work together need to get to know each other on a more personal basis.[2] This practice goes against a predominant paradigm in US organizations in which some think your personal life and work life must be completely separate. I am not suggesting that you share your personal journals with each other; but, I do believe that sharing some things about yourself builds relationships and connectivity with other people. It is this connectivity, this web of interconnections and interrelationships, that supports a group's resilience when issues surface that challenge relationships, because they will have more investment in and support of each other when they know each other better.

Sharing about yourself builds relationships and connectivity with others.

Two participants in my study whose groups repaired broken trust offered these thoughts that reinforce the need to get to know people better:

> Tony: Trust is easy to develop if you are real and if you are willing to risk a little of who you are. Build relationships—human interaction is such an

important component of trust. Sometimes we are so focused on doing or getting the business that we fail to remember that people do business with people they trust.

James: We do all of our meetings virtually, via phone and stuff. I always opened the meeting with ice breaker kind of things. I just tried to build the relationships. It is very interesting. We have people from different cultures. When you find out things about others that are so foreign from other people that when you listen to them, you see them on a different basis. People who lived in other countries, or those who couldn't afford to go to school, those that didn't work as teenagers, and those who had their first jobs with a paper route. You see them as more valued members of the team after that because people have new interests in each other and something in common. It builds relationships.

One of my favorite activities designed to strengthen relationships and foster trust begins with introducing the Johari Window and moves into activities that deepen understanding of other people. I explain the model and invite participants to share one unique thing about themselves with someone sitting next to them. The activity always energizes the room because human beings are wired for connectivity, and I believe we long for deeper connections together whether people are conscious about that or not. I have written more about the Johari Window tool and a process for you to use in chapter 10. Whether you use a tool or just host a conversation,

> "The meeting of two personalities is like the contact of two chemical substances: if there is any reaction, both are transformed."
> —Carl Jung

getting to know others is an important step in repairing trust in groups and a solid investment in your team's resilience for the future.

Seek Feedback

Repairing relationships also relies on whether a group can give and receive feedback that is meaningful and useful. I have found that people do not do this well—not because of insincerity or lack of trying to do it right, but because they need better understanding of the principles of feedback. I believe this stems from fear about not harming relationships, egos interfering with accepting feedback, and a general ignorance about how to give and receive feedback.

A client of mine, Russell, really wanted his manager to take action on feedback he was giving him. He believed the manager was too focused on larger projects outside to appreciate the hard work of his frontline staff within his department. Russell gave feedback and suggestions during meetings with his boss about how he experienced his management style within the department. He provided specific information about particular staff doing exceptional work so all the boss had to do was read it out loud and publicly recognize that work. Russell kept emailing his boss with the hope that he would take this feedback and do something. It did not happen. Russell's hopes that his feedback would make the top manager understand the need to recognize and appreciate his employees deflated.

Here are some things you need to know about feedback:[3]

1. Feedback *always* says something about the giver. The information provided may have more to do with the giver than the receiver.
2. Feedback is information. If you characterize feedback as information, it depersonalizes it. It becomes less about people liking or disliking you and allows you to sort through the information and find the gem for you.

3. The receiver chooses what to do with the feedback. As the recipient of the feedback, it is always the receiver's choice whether they accept or reject the feedback.

4. The giver must let go of the feedback once given away. You cannot hold on to the hope or expectation that the recipient will do anything with your feedback. Do not get emotionally tied to your feedback because your ego is involved. Remember that your feedback says a lot about what you want and need. Often, your identity is connected to the feedback you give to others. If the recipient does not like or use the feedback, you must learn to separate that choice from personal feelings about you.

As I explained these four pieces about feedback to Russell, he experienced an aha moment. He decided to let go of his hope and expectation that his manager would do anything with his feedback. It was simply not in his personality or management style, and Russell clearly was not going to change him. Instead, he shifted his energy to find ways to help the line staff know they were appreciated in an effort to keep morale up. While the manger appeared to not comprehend his impact on his department employees, Russell believed that learning about feedback lifted his burden and that helped.

> *If you do not know your impact on others, you are not paying attention. There is information all around you because the system is always giving you feedback.*

Feedback is essential for monitoring progress and it allows you to gauge your impact on others. If you do not know your impact on others, you are not paying attention. There is information all around you because the system is always giving you feedback. The manager in Russell's story either did not know or appear to care about his impact on the group. The gift of feedback is that it is always available to you because the system is always giving you feedback. Do people respond when you ask questions? Do others listen to your opinion? Do you feel welcome when you attend meetings? What are the nonverbal communication messages you see? There are many signals of feedback that you should pay attention to so that you understand your impact on others. Not paying attention signals that you do not care or may be afraid to find out more. Also, if you appear to be paying attention but are really multitasking, looking at your mobile device, or are otherwise distracted, you are clearly sending a message to others that they are not important.

Comprehensive Remedies

The first two phases of the Trust Repair Model should inform you about the core issues facing the group. If understanding, acknowledging, and apologizing do not fix the problems, then you need to make sure you engage in a comprehensive set of activities to remedy each of the main issues. My study found that groups that repaired trust had repair strategies that generally responded to most or all the identified trust issues. In fact, successful remedies covered more areas than the original violations identified.

Table 1 illustrates comparisons between the nature of the violation and the nature of the repair attempt. The purpose of this table is to align the trust violations with the repair remedies. The details within the tables are less important than the significance of aligning actions to respond to the core issues. Where there are holes, there are problems.

One of my study's participants, Sadie, claimed that her team repaired trust. Sadie provided four main areas where trust was violated ("nature of trust violations" column). Notice that all four of Sadie's team's trust violations had remedies ("repair strategies" column). They also did one additional thing that focused on the supervisor seeking coaching to improve her leadership. This was not identified as a violation of trust; however, it was something extra that the supervisor worked on to improve relationships. While all these activities took place over the course of a year, Sadie reported that her team did repair trust.

Table 1: Comparison of the Violation and the Repair Strategies: Sadie

Nature of trust violations	Repair strategies
Discounting, disrespectful, rude behaviors	Intervention from an outside consultant helped each person see the value of each person's contributions and taught common problem-solving tools they could use together
Mistrust in how each other performed duties	Clarified roles, responsibilities, and straightened out process issues
Refusing to listen to each other	Listened to and explored each other's perspectives
Blaming each other	Acknowledgment and apologies from both sides
	Supervisor sought coaching to improve leadership style

Table 2 illustrates another study participant's experience, where the repair strategy matched the nature of the identified trust violations and Madi's team went beyond and did several other activities to make a difference in strengthening relationships. Madi also reported that her group repaired trust.

Table 2: Comparison of the Violation and the Repair Strategies: Madi

Nature of trust violations	Repair strategies
Breach of confidentiality	Rechartered team with clear expectations and consequences if confidentiality is broken
Person lied when confronted initially	Person acknowledged lying and offered sincere apology with explanations and remedies to not do it again

Nature of trust violations	Repair strategies
Violator wanted to be liked and changed her story, depending on whom she was talking to	Violator honored tasks and worked hard to restore trustworthiness with other team members (e.g. worked on consistency)
	Whole team discussion to clarify what happened
	Reflection period right after the violation occurred, spent time thinking about what to do, roles people played, acknowledgment, and how to move forward
	Renewed personal commitment by every team member toward purpose and support of each other

Let's explore the other side. Table 3 illustrates Brad's group activities. This group did not repair trust. There are some holes in the repair strategies. They did not match enough of the trust violations with appropriate repair strategies.

Table 3: Comparison of the Violation and the Repair Strategies: Brad

Nature of trust violations	Repair strategies
Did not listen to each other	Held retreats and one-on-one meetings to try and talk, listen, and plan goals, but it didn't work well
Dismissed, degraded people; constant rude and disrespectful behaviors	
Blamed others, no personal acknowledgment	
Meetings were long, unhelpful, and mismanaged	Improved meeting structure to manage times better

While Brad expressed that the group held retreats to plan goals and tried to listen to each other, some of the board members were still unwilling to accept that any of their behaviors were dismissive and rude. Without any acknowledgment (e.g., blaming others for the problems, not owning their part) or willingness to consider that behaviors were offensive to others, this major piece of the trust violations went unrepaired. While progress was made structurally on improving meetings, the meeting issue was not at the crux of the trust problems, and the group did not repair trust.

In another unsuccessful trust repair attempt, Mike shared that his organization experienced significant upheaval and changes in their pension plans, leadership structure, and treatment of employees.

Table 4: Comparison of the Violation and the Repair Strategies: Mike

Nature of trust violations	Repair strategies
Policy changes that affected livelihood (e.g., changes to retirement benefits)	Minimal response: funding issues and new board members made a strategic choice, but reasons were not communicated well to the organization
Psychological contract change (e.g., people believed they should get promotions instead of hiring outside)	
Change in management; key operational people not represented on leadership team anymore	
Perceived as not valuing long-term employees	Intervention: employee groups took photos that exemplified the mission and organizational values and shared it with each other

Nature of trust violations	Repair strategies
Leadership: wrong person and unclear intent communicated with major changes in organization	Leader was not present to give the message directly to employees during significant change

Table 4 illustrates that Mike's organization's efforts did not adequately address all the identified trust violations. Mike described a series of deep violations of trust, which included a significant personal toll from the changes happening within both the organization and the leadership team. The repair efforts left holes in responding to the psychological contract changes and leadership disconnect; even though some attempts were made by the leader to hold regular meetings with people, it was not enough to work through all the trust issues.

The details within the tables are less important than the significance of aligning actions to respond to the core issues. Where there are holes in the repair strategies, there are problems.

> ### Reflection Questions
> Use this table concept to help you design a comprehensive approach to repairing the trust issues within your group. Place the core issues in one column and evaluate what you have done so far in the repair strategies column. Are there any holes?

To deepen a comprehensive response in repairing trust, Hong Ren and Barbara Gray conceptualized the process as one that honors the cultures each party comes from, acknowledges the violation type, and embarks on a set of rituals for restoration that align with all three elements.[4] This means that you need to tailor the repair activities to match the cultural needs of the people and the group.

To be effective, your repair activities should look different in a non-profit organization than they would in an educational institution, a government entity, or a private sector business. What may work at a global corporation will need to be tailored differently to support a small family-owned farm business. Repair activities must reflect understanding of the culture of the people involved, the group norms, and other practices that honor the group's identity. Think about how gender, age, ability, race, ethnicity, and so on also impact the design of your repair activities. The more sensitive and intentional you are, the better the probability for a favorable outcome.

To demonstrate the power of cultural rituals, one participant in my study reported a core values exercise that went very well. The exercise helped to realign people with the purpose of the nonprofit organization:

> Mike: I had them break into four groups and sent them out with a camera and told them to take pictures of things that they observed that epitomized their organization. There couldn't be any people in the pictures. When they came back with their digital photos, I had them explain to the group why that picture epitomized their experience. And it opened a lot of eyes about people's emotional attachment to the organization and how they were feeling given the violations of trust that were going on. That experience was incredible.

People attracted to work at nonprofit or public organizations are typically grounded in service to others and compelled to work toward a higher purpose or mission. Repair activities need to consider the benevolence and connection people feel to their cause and the clients they serve.

I worked for government for eighteen years, and the public sector continues to be a client of mine. I believe there is a connection to mission for people here, too, but there is also need for stability and security. Citizens count on government to be there for a safety net and provide services to vulnerable populations, and when government is working at its best, it is behind the scenes keeping things working. While I might use some of the same kinds of activities with nonprofit and government clients, I tailor the approach to suit their unique needs and group characteristics.

Private sector organizations have a different kind of pace and tenor and are driven by a different kind of service—certainly a strong focus to provide value to their customers and shareholders. Demonstrating how these activities affect the bottom line or their efficiency in working together must be a part of any activities designed to help teams repair trust together in the private sector.

If you conduct decent analysis in the Reflect phase of this model, then you will have considered the organizational needs and influences on the trust situation (systems thinking). Use that knowledge to determine and design activities that will honor your group's unique characteristics in the Repair phase. While I offer a model and several tools to consider using in your repair activities, no one recipe exists to repair trust in groups. Instead, you might consider all these activities and choices to be your ingredients, and you are the chef who decides what goes in, how much, how long something gets worked on, and when you think it is done. Great chefs work on a recipe for years until they believe it is ready. This level of tenacity is what it takes to repair trust in groups. It takes time to tailor activities that address the key issues, and it can take several iterations of these activities to reach a healthy level of trust. Clients and study participants of mine have done it...and you can do it, too!

Step 6: Create Agreements

After engaging in several kinds of repair activities, your group may find that it needs to make new agreements addressing how you will operate and relate with each other as you move forward. Creating agreements strengthens the structural foundation of a group. In my study, structural issues were not initially considered as problems contributing to a group's violations of trust. People failed to realize that structure was a huge contributing factor to their trust issues. This is why the Trust Behaviors Framework begins with purpose, progresses to roles, and then to core processes.

New or revised agreements can positively impact group trust repair in several ways:

- Clarify the mission, vision, values, and goals
- Create group or project charter agreements
- Determine roles and responsibilities
- Clarify sponsorship
- Design new or improved strategies
- Improve processes clarifying roles
- Determine deliverables and generate expectations of core work processes
- Renew or set team ground rules or rules of engagement

Participants who claimed that their group had repaired trust used repair activities that included creating agreements and structural components such as clarifying processes, roles, and responsibilities. Several reported using a charter document and either updating it to reflect the necessary changes or creating a new one. Some spent time simplifying or translating their work, which led to increased understanding and improved trust relations.

> Sadie: We weren't really looking at interpersonal conflict. That's what it seemed to us, but what it really was, was unclear roles, processes, and responsibilities. So, knowing that, we could shift to "OK, what do we need to do?" And that really helped.

> Collette: We decided to get together to improve the process. We identified the needs that the current process wasn't meeting and incorporated those into

it and fixed the breaks that were in the process. We clearly spelled out steps and made rules and consequences to support it.

Madi: We went back to the charter and we signed off on it again. We would follow the meeting rules, communication aspects, etc. Basically, give her another chance. The chair said if this happened to anyone else (a breach of trust that they were repairing) that we would do the same thing.

Sujul: We didn't have an agenda, and we needed to have a charter so that we were clear about what had to be done. Even if it was a simple, two sentences or whatever, we would make sure we knew what needed to be done and could be on the same page.

Of the participants in my study who claimed that their group did not repair trust, only 8 percent created agreements in their attempt to remedy the situation. These participants reported that personal agendas, lack of process management, willingly choosing to not follow a process or rule, unclear roles or responsibilities, proposing solutions before gathering data, and having no charter-type agreements in place all contributed to the trust violations. Even knowing the nature of the violations, 92 percent did not do anything about re-creating or adjusting agreements. This reinforces the message that once you get clear about the core of the trust issues, you need to do something about each area and not forget the importance of the initial structural agreements that every group needs to be successful.

In this important work of creating agreements, remember to not get wrapped up with too many details. If someone lets a group down by missing an important deadline, do not create a series of additional steps for that individual to guarantee the issue will not reoccur. This causes the focus to shift from the missed deadline and its impact on the group to whether the person does all the new steps as promised. These steps can also be perceived as punishment. And punishing people is not a way to build trust.

The key is to spend adequate time and make sure people understand the reasons for the new or updated agreements, ensure they have a voice in determining those agreements, and make sure the agreements are clear to everyone involved. Extensive details that result in excessive time dedicated to drafting, reading, editing, revising, and interpreting may not be an effective use of time and can often lead to additional problems. If the emphasis on repairing trust centers too heavily on the details of the agreements, rather than a combination of understanding the reasons for the agreements and the agreements themselves, people will focus their energy on simply the monitoring details. When this happens, relationships and work suffer.

While coaching two different groups through trust repair activities centered on breaches of confidentiality problems, the importance of focus clearly emerged. One group chose to hold a meeting where every member discussed the confidentiality issue, and they spent time making sure everyone knew the impact of those actions. Over a couple of meetings, they generated some new working agreements around how to handle information requests and renewed their ground rules. This group did very well moving forward because people knew the reasons for the new agreements and all had a say in creating them.

The second group I worked with chose a different path. The leader and one other member essentially decided what the new rules were going to be and laid it out in a meeting with a procedures document placed on their intranet shared folder. It included details about who would have access to the confidential information, outlined a process for requesting privileges to see the confidential information, and even specified a subject line format for email. After that, if a group member made a mistake on the email subject line or the procedures to request information, the discussion centered on the details of their missteps. Then it became group in-fighting around the details stating they were not clear, fair, or efficient.

These two examples raise the question: do you want to spend time focusing on the procedural details, or do you want to spend time helping people understand that when they breach confidentiality it hurts the whole group? You must have an appropriate balance of both: providing clear guidance so that people know what is expected of them and spending enough time helping people understand why creating or renewing agreements is necessary.

I have one final thought to offer you to achieve success in the Repair phase of this Trust Repair Model. You might conduct some repair activities yourself, but if you find that it is not addressing all the issues, you may need to solicit outside help and input from people trained to lead groups through conflict management, change facilitation, and/or mediation. These people should have additional tools and models to guide you through the process of repairing relationships and improving operations.

Summary

The third phase of the Trust Repair Model, Repair, utilizes a variety of activities uniquely designed to help your group repair the key issues that you identified in the Understand and Reflect phases. Step 5 in the Trust Repair Model uses an action research approach where you start with a baseline, engage in activities to improve trust, seek feedback, assess the impact, and repeat as necessary. Giving and receiving feedback will be an important skill that your group needs to develop to bring about a level of honesty and help your group improve.

Step 5 is most successful when groups take a comprehensive approach responding to the identified core trust issues. When there are holes in the strategy or if any key issue is not addressed, the likelihood of repairing trust diminishes.

Once activities have enabled the group to work through their trust issues, agreements may need to be recorded so that everyone is clear about expectations. Creating agreements is step 6 in the model. Be mindful about balancing the need for clear documentation with ensuring that group members understand the need for documentation as a remedy to strengthen the structural components of trust.

Further Your Learning and Use of the Model

I offer two sets of practical tools to further your learning.

- Activities to deepen understanding: At the end of this chapter you will find individual reflection questions and short assignments designed to deepen your understanding of the chapter content.
- Repair tools: In chapter 10 I have provided some tools with descriptions of how to use them with individuals or in groups. Most tools are coupled with a real example of using the tool with a group or individual to aid in your learning and understanding of how to use and adapt the tool to your trust situation. The intention is to give you immediate tools to support working with repairing trust in your group.
  - Johari Window
  - Values Table
  - Team Charter

Activities to Deepen Understanding

Reflection Questions

Think about the last time you received feedback from someone.
What was the feedback?

REPAIR

Engage in
Repair
Activities

Seek
Feedback

Gauge
Progress

Did you consider the feedback to be positive? Corrective action? Other?

Create
Agreements

How did the feedback affect you?

Did you act on the feedback? Do anything with it?

How did the feedback relate to these four points (listed below) about feedback? Make notes about your experience.

1. Feedback *always* says something about the giver.
2. Feedback is information.
3. The receiver chooses what to do with the feedback.
4. The giver must let go of the feedback once given away.

Now, think about the next time you will provide feedback. How can you improve your feedback skills? What would this look like?

CHAPTER 7

Evolve

Having looked the past in the eye, having asked for forgiveness and having made amends, let us shut the door on the past—not in order to forget it but in order to not allow it to imprison us.
—Desmond Tutu

Repairing trust takes courage and a mindset that human beings can evolve and change. Whether a group can repair and sustain trust becomes a question of intention. Do you and the other members of the group want to repair trust? How does it serve you to hold on to the past or relive the hurt that stemmed from the violations of trust? I found that if people will not fully engage or believe the situation can change, the effectiveness of repair activities diminishes and so does the possibility of repairing trust.

Step 7: Move Forward

One of the first things about moving forward is deciding to let go of reliving the past. It is natural to be hypersensitive to people who hurt you or the group. You may remain cautious when relating to those people, even if they have acknowledged and apologized for the actions that caused the trust violation. You may also be consciously or unconsciously looking for new examples to illustrate their failure to live up to the new agreements. Do not play the gotcha game. Handle setbacks with humor, steadfastness, empathy, and a willingness to help that person stay on track. You, too, will occasionally mess up and will want your peers to be just as gracious and forgiving to you. Moving forward includes learning how to let yourself and others grow and evolve as human beings; people are perfectly imperfect.

EVOLVE

Move Forward

Forgive

Learn, Grow and Evolve

Honor Agreements

Appreciate

It took several years for me to become better at not interrupting people. It was a hard habit to break, and frankly, I still occasionally interrupt others even though I try very hard not to. I do not want it thrown back at me as a sign that I am breaking trust if I slip back into an old habit or make a mistake.

> "Forget the failures, keep the lessons."
> —The Dalai Lama

Certain habits and behaviors can interfere with effective relationships. When people vow to improve, allow them ample time to actually adjust their behaviors. If someone slips up, instead of thinking, *See, she did it again; now I can never trust her*, work directly with this person and propose in a supportive, assertive, and empathic way: "Well, you did it again. Let's help you get back on track." There must be more understanding and patience as people grow, evolve, and change. You should anticipate slip-ups and discuss how to deal with mistakes and setbacks in a way that honors and supports relationships as part of your group agreement process.

You must make a choice to learn from the past and look to the future with more positivity and resilience. Barbara Fredrickson and Michele Tugade study the effects of positive emotions and resilience on personal and organizational health. Resilience is the ability to bounce back from negative emotional experiences and flexible adaptation to the changing demands of stressful experiences.[1] Resilient people who use positive emotions and find positive meaning in stressful encounters bounce back from these experiences quickly and effectively.

> *Resilience is the ability to bounce back from negative emotional experiences and flexible adaptation to the changing demands of stressful experiences.*
> — Barbara Fredrickson and Michele Tugade

Support Systems

To develop healthy resilience, you should cultivate strong support systems as individuals and as a group. Support systems are other people who can guide, encourage, or directly help you attain a desired goal (e.g., trust repair). Mentors of mine, Charles "Charlie" Seashore and Edith "Edie" Whitfield Seashore, were strong advocates for creating healthy support systems. They found that the ability to develop support systems is crucial to effective change management for two reasons.[2]

> *"Everybody needs support! Change in human systems is never created alone."*
> —Edie and Charlie Seashore

First, change will occur when the support for that change reaches critical mass among the members of that group. More than one person must want the change for it to work. The Seashores' work supported planned change in groups; which is conscious and intentional. This equates to the Repair phase, step 6 (create agreements) and step 7 (move forward and honor those agreements needed to repair trust). The success of your trust repair efforts depends on your ability to develop empowering partnerships across a full range of people.

Second, helping any group through change or repairing trust is a daunting task. Those who choose to take on this task must develop strong support systems. Change in human systems is never created alone; support systems are required. An initial support system might be one or two confidants. This small informal group might evolve into a larger group willing to take direct action and contribute to the critical mass that is crucial to success. Develop support systems to help you strategize and operationalize your change and trust repair strategy. Call on people to support you when you or the group feel challenged, apathetic, or discouraged. Finding a strong network of support is another way to sustain your repair efforts in the Evolve phase.

Forgiveness

Forgiveness helps repair trust because it builds on the belief that the violator not only accepts responsibility for what was done wrong but sincerely regrets it and is committed to not repeat it. Forgiveness does not mean pardoning, condoning, excusing, forgetting, or denying. It enables you to move forward without holding people hostage to their mistakes or violations of trust. Forgiveness ultimately becomes an emotional and cognitive release for you and for others.

> *Forgiving: "To cease to feel resentment"*
> *Forgive: "Allowing room for error or weakness"*
> —Merriam-Webster Collegiate Dictionary

Robert Enright, who has studied forgiveness for years, asserts that forgiveness can lead to more orderly thinking, feeling, and acting.[3] Holding on to resentment and bitterness not only harms you; it flows outward to your group and affects relationships and work processes. Enright offered that a major goal of forgiveness is reconciliation, but that does not always work. He further explained that "It is not necessary to reconcile if the other person is a danger to you. It may be necessary to remove yourself from any physical proximity from this person to preclude further hurt. Forgiveness does not mean you are a punching bag."[4]

There are barriers to forgiveness that should be considered. On the violator's side, there may be fear of punishment or restrictions, or shame associated with acknowledging guilt.[5] You should anticipate some of these fears and be ready to address them and support people as they face the difficult emotions that come along with it. If this is not handled well, people

> "We must develop and maintain the capacity to forgive. He who is devoid of the power to forgive is devoid of the power to love."
> —Rev. Dr. Martin Luther King Jr.

will put up barriers to protect themselves, which further closes off communication and the ability to strengthen relationships.

Some people are overly harsh on themselves and it affects their ability to self-forgive. Self-berating and overly critical thinking are symptoms that become problems from the inability to let go, learn, and move on. People in this category also need support and patience to help them explore the gift of reframing. Reframing takes an experience and allows you to shift your mindset. For example, whenever I am stuck in traffic and I get grumpy about the loss of time,

> "People who refuse to admit mistakes can never receive the gift of forgiveness."
> —Molly Drescher

my daughter Maren reminds me: "Well, it is just more time you get to spend with me!" The first time she said that to me, my whole demeanor changed from gripping the steering wheel and sighing heavily to laughing and enjoying the moment with her in the car. A reframe can take a frustrating moment and turn it into something fun, or a mistake and make it a learning experience.

From the forgiver's side, there may be fears that the violations will be repeated or that if they forgive, they may appear weak. There may be a loss of victim status, and justice may not be fully served. It becomes a personal decision point: what is gained by forgiving someone, and what is lost? These concerns tend to be centered around identity and core beliefs about justice. Do not treat these concerns lightly, because they are replete with people's life experiences. People in this category need patience, support, and reframing strategies too. Reframe *victim* to another word that is more powerful such as *driver, advocate, learner,* or *controller.* Help the person find the right word to replace the one that keeps them stuck.

Here is an example from one of my participants in my trust study that sums up the Evolve Phase nicely:

> Abigale: I can't say that everybody is in exactly the same place that they were before this happened. And I don't think that is realistic to think, but we have found other ways of trusting and we are able work with each other. And understanding that what happens is in the past, really is the past. Up until now it has been this way and now we have an opportunity to do something different.

Summary

The fourth and final phase of the Trust Repair Model is Evolve. After working through various repair efforts with your group, people must be allowed to learn, grow, and change as human beings. You must not hold people hostage to the time when they made mistakes or contributed to the violations of trust. It takes intentionality to want to move forward, and if people do not want to, the likelihood of truly repairing trust diminishes. Evolving also requires forgiveness and healthy support systems.

Forgiveness is deeply rooted in the emotional psyche, and everyone approaches it differently. Forgiveness does not mean you approve of the violations that occurred. Rather, forgiveness is about releasing yourself from reexperiencing the pain and allows others to grow into better people. You will find that practicing forgiveness is another way to support healthy trust repair in groups.

To do this, create strong systems of people who can guide, offer support, and serve as back-up to you and the group. Slip ups will happen, so being prepared for setbacks and challenges with grace, humor, and patience will serve you and the group well. The Evolve Phase is about sustaining the work you have done up to this point and adjusting strategies as you move to the future.

Further Your Learning and Use of the Model

I offer two sets of practical tools to further your learning.

- Activities to deepen understanding: At the end of this chapter you will find individual reflection questions and short assignments designed to deepen your understanding of the chapter content.
- Evolve tools: In chapter 10 I have provided two tools with descriptions of how to use them with individuals or in groups. Most tools are coupled with a real example of using the tool with a group or individual to aid in your learning and understanding of how to use and adapt the tool to your trust situation. The intention is to give you immediate tools to support working with repairing trust in your group.
  - Check-Ins and Check-Outs
  - Evaluation

Activities to Deepen Understanding

Reflection Questions

What are the most important lessons you learned after making a mistake or experiencing a failure?

EVOLVE

Move Forward

Forgive

Learn, Grow and Evolve

Honor Agreements

Appreciate

Have you noticed any patterns in how you react to your own mistakes or failures? If so, what are those patterns?

What beliefs do you hold regarding forgiveness?

Do you forgive yourself? If so, how do you do it? Do you let go of the event after you processed it and have forgiven yourself?

What is it like for you to forgive others? Under what circumstances is forgiving others easy or difficult for you? Why?

Short Assignment: Personal Support Systems

EVOLVE

Move
Forward

Forgive

Learn,
Grow
and Evolve

Honor
Agreements

Appreciate

Human relationships serve a variety of important functions that help to keep us human. A support system is a selectively drawn resource pool to support me to move in a direction of my choice and makes me stronger.

Please read the descriptions below, then enter the names of the people in your life who provide that function in your relationships with them. Think of friends, family, coworkers, or other individuals in your life who can provide you with support.

Types of Personal Support	Names
Role models: People you admire, respect, see as competent and confident. People you would like to be like in one or many respects.	
Social integrators: People who share your concerns because they are in the same boat. People who are striving for similar goals and with whom you share experiences, ideas, favors.	
Relaxers: People who provide you with warmth and closeness. Those with whom you share feelings freely and without self-consciousness.	
Dependables: People who can be depended upon in a crisis. Those who provide personal assistance or make things available to you and always seem to be easy to ask for help when you have a problem.	
Respecters: People who respect your competence and who understand the difficulty and value of your work. People you respect and who recognize your skills and give you self-worth.	

Types of Personal Support	Names
Referral agents: People who are linking pins to needed resources. Those you turn to when you are faced with not knowing who or what can be helpful in a situation.	
Challengers: People who make you stretch, give other perspectives, challenge your assumptions and working principles, stretch you to move in new directions, ask you things you have not considered.	
Guides: People who provide you with advice and methods to solve problems. People who help you identify steps in solving problems, achieving goals, and taking action.	

Source: Charles Seashore

Questions

Review the names in your support system.
Do you have a strong support system?

Where are you missing support?

Do you have one individual in three or more categories? Are you overly reliant on this person?

How can you build your support system to achieve your goal?

Who are people you can add to your support system?

Are you resisting support in an area? If so, why?

What are your next steps to acknowledging and building your support system to achieve your personal goals?

Nonhuman Supports

Animals, music, exercise, technology, books, nature, and hobbies can be an important part of your support system. Keep them in mind as you assess what you have and what is missing.

Adapted from Michael Broom, Edith Seashore, and Gwen Kennedy. Used with permission.

CHAPTER 8
Success Factors

When they go low, we go high.
—Michelle Obama

What differentiates groups that repair trust from those that do not? My research revealed seven significant factors that successful groups did to repair trust.[1] As you read and reflect on these areas, think about how you can proactively work with groups to preempt issues that threaten trust. Each factor below offers solid leadership advice to help groups strengthen their capacity to handle challenges to trust and work through them.

Intentionally Engage

For those groups that repaired trust, the way people engaged in their work was more significant and sophisticated. People were intentional about how they listened, considered the situation, received feedback, and engaged with each other in dialogue. They were conscious that they each played a part in how things unraveled and that they each must play a part in the repair. And they were authentically willing to do the hard work.

People displayed a level of professionalism and respect, even with those who had violated the trust. They were willing to investigate what had occurred and were willing to work through it. This level of sophistication and intentionality is truly remarkable. The level of openness to explore the situation and consider all sides of the story and the ability to give and receive feedback set these groups apart from the groups that did not repair trust. It is important to note that the groups that did not repair trust expressed a desire to have this level of openness, too. Despite their best attempts, it was not well received or it was disregarded.

It is important to discern if people are merely going through the motions of engaging in trust repair but not really interested in doing it. Some people are unwilling to try because it is too painful or they have given up hope that anything will change. If leaders are not on board, no one will respect the process. Others are unwilling or unable to acknowledge their impact because they cannot see past their belief that it is the other person's fault. These folks keep the mindset that others should change in order to repair trust, not themselves. If they remain unwilling to see that they can do something about it, then trust repair efforts are thwarted. The key question that must be answered is, Do they *want* to repair trust?

As a consultant, I find that working with clients who are intentional and willing to do the work they have hired me to do is rewarding. And the inverse is true. When I sense or learn they are unwilling to do the real work, I have a choice to make. Unless they become willing participants, it is futile to continue facilitating the trust repair process.

Allow Ample Time

Remember, people must be ready and willing to make things better. Sometimes they are not ready right away, and a cooling-off period may be needed. And let's be real: it has likely taken a lot of time to get to where they are, and it is going to take more than one hour to repair. Taking time to think

Most research participants expressed that it took six to thirty-six months to repair trust.

about the situation, through reflection or just pausing long enough to let the emotions settle, seemed to make a difference for groups that repaired trust. Most research participants expressed that it took six to thirty-six months to repair trust.

It takes time to repair a trust violation, and it is naïve to think it can be fixed in a meeting or one off-site retreat. Several of the participants whose groups did not repair trust believed they did not spend enough time on repair efforts. Organizations that track billable hours or other productivity ratios must adjust and allow people to have ample time to invest in repair efforts.

Responding to trust issues quickly enough was a theme for both the groups that repaired trust and those that did not. Strong emotions like resentment can possibly be cleared up through an immediate conversation to help clarify the issues, check in on intent, and work to resolve it. If left to fester, however, resentment and other strong emotions can turn to anger. As people become angrier, they become less willing to work on repair strategies. When emotions spike, people no longer have full use of their brains, because anger and fear trigger the fight-or-flight mechanism. Taking ample time to allow emotions to calm down and work through the intricacies of repairing trust is critical.

Own It: Acknowledge, Apologize, and Move Forward

People who repair trust own their part. They acknowledge, apologize, do the work, and move forward. Blame or self-deprecation does not help. Groups that repair trust tend to explore, learn, and move forward. In other words, they do not hold on to the past, but that does not mean they forget about the experience, either. They have a more mature way of evaluating the experience, learning from it, repairing, and moving forward by making new agreements. It is a choice. Members of the groups that did not repair trust tended to stay stuck, not forgive others, and evade ownership of their part in the situation.

Persevere

Groups that repair trust have a level of tenacity, grit, and persever-ance. They stick with it even when it gets hard or uncomfortable. Trust repair can be messy. It is not a linear road to improvement, and consequently, some groups experience setbacks. Successful groups try a strategy, and if it does not work or a participant does not honor the latest agreement, they immediately recognize it and want to try again. They move forward and do not just say, "Whatever." They keep trying to improve the situation because they have a stake in it. They care. They care about the team, its purpose, and making life better within that group. This does not mean they are trying to become best friends, but if they plan to continue working together on the team, it makes sense to continue working on trust repair.

Resilient people who use positive emotions and find positive meaning in stressful encounters bounce back from

> There is no finish line.
> —Nike slogan

these experiences quickly and effectively.[1] There is a sense of resil-iency in the stories of the groups that repaired trust. They perse-vered when it was most difficult, they had hope, and they believed things could get better and kept working on it until it did.

Invest in People

Spending time building the right team and continuing to invest in their development pays off. Period. Groups that successfully repair trust draw upon the knowledge, skills, and abilities of their people. They spend time and resources developing these people so that the right set of tools can be leveraged when needed.

Having a common knowledge base of personality theory (e.g. Myers Briggs Type Indicator), common problem-solving (e.g. *Crucial Conversations, Immunity to Change, Five Dysfunctions of a Team*), and communication models supports a group's ability to work on issues. Providing training and development for employees and leaders does not always mean they use it well or right away; however, it is clear that it makes a difference in repair efforts because people have a common learning experience and use it when needed.

The study also found that if training is provided too late, if too much damage has been done, then the likelihood of the training serving as a helpful tool in the repair process is lowered. For example, one participant in my study stated that he took his group on a retreat and tried to facilitate different ways to open-up the conversation, but he believed the opinions were too entrenched and the damage was too far gone, therefore, his group did not repair trust.

Practice Effective Leadership

Leaders play a very important role in repair efforts. Leaders provide multiple strategies to support the repair process within their groups. They clarify roles and responsibilities, listen and communicate well, and show empathy by demonstrating care regarding welfare of people all while moving the group closer to achieving positive results. Put the right people in leadership positions. Effective leadership makes a difference in whether groups recover from setbacks and trust violations.

It was disconcerting to hear stories from participants regarding their perceptions of the depth of ineffective leadership. To illustrate this point, George described trying to explain a critical situation at a job site to his supervisor. The supervisor wanted him to do something, and George was adamant it was wrong from a safety perspective. This supervisor became so angry that he picked up a piece of wood and threw it at George, missing him physically but clearly hitting him with disregard and disrespect. In another group, Hector also pointed out that when he and his fellow project teammates expressed any kind of feedback to the junior partner (their supervisor), they were punished with more menial work. And Monique offered: "Instead of perpetuating gossip, two of us actually went and talked to our supervisor about it. And you know what, he laughed about it. And it continued."

Offer Comprehensive Remedies

The key for those participants whose groups were successful in trust repair appeared to be in the breadth and alignment of the repair strategies. The study found that groups that repaired trust had repair strategies that generally responded to most or all the identified trust issues. In fact, successful remedies covered more areas than the original violations identified. The tables in chapter 6 illustrate this point.

Organizations and Groups Need Structure

There was one surprise in my study as it relates to trust repair remedies. Structural issues were not generally perceived initially as a trust violation by the people I interviewed, yet many times it was a key influence on the conditions that led to the violation occurring. Structural issues are defined as anything that can be written down and explicitly provided to others to shape work and even outline expected core behaviors (e.g., team charters that express team norms). Structural issues include processes, roles, responsibilities, policies, procedures, contracts, charters, and other agreements.

Several of the groups that repaired trust seemed to improve, clarify, or create structural remedies to help reinforce their trust agreements. For example, one group had outside forces influencing their core processes that were leaving their roles and responsibilities unclear. The unclear roles and responsibilities influenced the behaviors from members of the team, and those behaviors were the ones originally identified as leading and causing trust issues. The interesting thing was that the structural issue of outside forces affecting core work processes leading to unclear roles and responsibilities was not initially seen as a core violation of trust. Yet, through the help of an outside consultant, the group could see that the underlying structural issues of role uncertainty were more of a culprit in the erosion of trust than the personalities and behaviors of individuals. It was because of the underlying structural issues that the unwelcomed behaviors showed up and compromised trust among team members.

Among the groups that did not repair trust, there were only a few who identified structural issues as either a core violation of trust or as a condition that affected or influenced the violation. For example, one group specifically talked about changes to a core process that made things worse and further violated trust. Clearly they needed to do something about it. While it was recognized as a core problem, leaders refused to do anything about it. Because there was no change to the process, the structural violation of trust in this story was not resolved and the group did not repair trust.

Summary

In my trust repair study, I found some distinct factors that separated the groups that repaired trust from those that did not. These seven success factors are:

1. Intentionally engage: group members were intentional about engaging in the process; they wanted to repair trust and strengthen relationships.

2. Allow ample time: repairing trust takes time; the average was six to thirty-six months for groups that successfully repaired trust.

3. Own it: people acknowledged and owned their part and did not try to circumvent responsibility.

4. Persevere: even when it got difficult, people stuck it out and reaped the benefit of repaired relationships.

5. Invest in people: it pays to invest in training and development with groups before they need to use communication, conflict, and problem-solving to repair relationships.

6. Practice effective leadership: whoever sits in the leadership position matters if the group is going to successfully repair trust.

7. Offer comprehensive remedies: groups identified the core issues affecting trust and engaged in multiple activities to address the core issues without missing anything significant.

CHAPTER 9
What If Others Do Not Want to Repair?

Life's challenges are not supposed to paralyze you. They are supposed to help you discover who you are.
— Bernice Johnson Reagon

Sometimes, people are just not willing to participate in repairing trust, no matter how compelling the operational and personal reasons are or how hard you try. These people simply do not believe they have anything to work on, and their unwillingness probably stems from a mindset that it is others who need to change. When this happens, do not lose hope; they may be ready to discuss repairing the relationships at some point in the future. In the meantime, you do not need to be held back by their lack of participation. There are strategies and mindset adjustments that can assist you in working through the Trust Repair Model by yourself and can offer some relief.

Remember that you cannot change other people or force them to be something they are not. As much as you want them to be kind, open, transparent, reliable, professional, or whatever you yearn for them to be, they may not have the skills, abilities, or desire to be anything different than what they are right now. The first

> *The first mindset adjustment is for you: stop trying to make other people change, because it is wasted energy.*

mindset adjustment is for you: stop trying to make other people change, because it is wasted energy. The only changes that you can guarantee are those that you personally make yourself. You can adjust your role, core work processes, communication patterns, and interpersonal dynamics that reflect the changes you want.

Stop Your Wasted Energy Cycle

It is frustrating to get caught up in a wasted energy cycle of hoping that others will change, especially when they do not. You may feel incapable of moving forward without their buy-in. To illustrate, if a co-worker continuously fails to understand that their lack of follow-through is adversely affecting you and the group's core process work, you have some choices to make.

This image demonstrates the wasted energy cycle. It begins as Person A lacks follow-through. That lack of follow-through affects the timeliness of the group's work. When the work is late, everyone in the group is affected (people become frustrated, the quality of work diminishes, people take on additional work to cover for Person A's lack of follow-through). People then should provide feedback and reaffirm expectations with Person A. Person A continues to not follow through, resulting in the group members becoming more frustrated. The cycle continues.

Wasted Energy Cycle

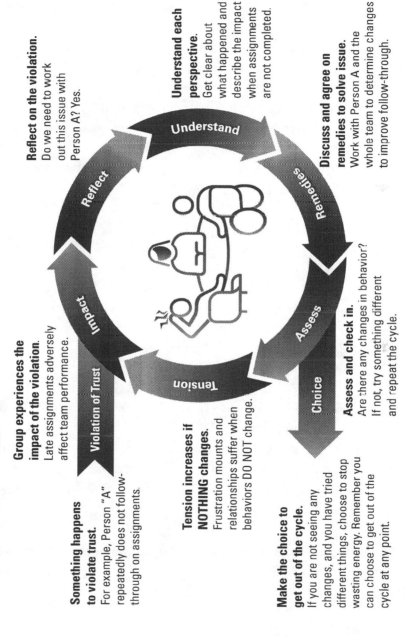

Reflect on the violation. Do we need to work out this issue with Person A? Yes.

Understand each perspective. Get clear about what happened and describe the impact when assignments are not completed.

Discuss and agree on remedies to solve issue. Work with Person A and the whole team to determine changes to improve follow-through.

Group experiences the impact of the violation. Late assignments adversely affect team performance.

Something happens to violate trust. For example, Person "A" repeatedly does not follow-through on assignments.

Tension increases if NOTHING changes. Frustration mounts and relationships suffer when behaviors DO NOT change.

Make the choice to get out of the cycle. If you are not seeing any changes, and you have tried different things, choose to stop wasting energy. Remember you can choose to get out of the cycle at any point.

Assess and check in. Are there any changes in behavior? If not, try something different and repeat the cycle.

Cycle labels: Understand · Remedies · Assess · Choice · Tension · Impact · Violation of Trust · Reflect

How do you get out of the wasted energy cycle? Make different choices. You have several places to make a different choice that will better serve you. Presuming you have worked through the Reflect and Understand phases of the Trust Repair Model by giving feedback, clarifying expectations, reviewing responsibilities, checking in, and inquiring about what may be contributing to the lack of follow-through, generate different options to get a better result. Ask yourself: Why am I letting this person continuously let me down by not following through? What choices do I have to get a different result? The answer is *plenty*, but you must let go of any fears or concerns about making a different choice.

> How do you get out of the wasted energy cycle? Make different choices.

Consider the following questions and strategies that support making different choices and allow you to escape the wasted energy cycle.

Judgment

Do you have any skewed judgment around the quality of the work and follow-through? Are you being too picky or lenient? Does the person understand what *quality* means or realize how the work affects the next step in the process? Does the person need training, better machines, stronger templates, or examples?

Consequences

Are there appropriate consequences for the lack of follow-through?

Assign

Do you have the right people in the right places? Assigning people to positions is an essential leadership function. Sometimes there is a mismatch between what is required and what the person can perform. If the job changes because of technology or customer demand, or there are time sensitivities to consider, some people may not be in the right positions to meet that demand. Leaders need to be intentional about which responsibilities to assign people so they can be successful, the group can achieve performance goals, and customers receive the desired results. They need to make sure people have access to training, have been trained properly, and have clear job expectations. Occasionally, leading also means moving people from positions that do not match their skill set.

Adjust Mindset

Do you need to adjust your mindset about moving people to match their knowledge, skills, and abilities to the position's needs? If the suggestions above just gave you heartburn, you might need to adjust your mindset about moving people. As a consultant, I see people who appear to be mismatched to the job they are trying to perform. What are the human and operational costs of keeping someone in a position where they are not performing well?

One manager tried for years to coach one of her supervisors to balance the people side of managing with her intense task focus. She would send work back if she did not like a document's format, leave notes on a person's desk if they were not there precisely at eight a.m., and call out mistakes in a public and embarrassing manner to prove a point. This supervisor's staff was miserable, and the annual employee satisfaction survey revealed a several-year trend downward. Her team members sought transfers to other departments or simply left the company because they hated the environment. These people were highly specialized bioengineers who were hard to replace because of the education and skills level required for the positions.

After years of trying to help this supervisor adjust her style (through activities such as training, coaching, and mentorship), it still did not work, and the reluctant manager made the choice to make a change. Over a two-week period, she explored different positions that did not require supervising people. She found some options, and together they made a better position selection for her style. Three years later, I checked in and found a happier group of people in the unit and a happier non-supervisor.

Fear

What are your greatest concerns or fears that prevent you from moving away from the wasted energy cycle? Does it have to do with keeping relationship harmony in the group? Do you really have harmony if someone is not pulling their weight? I find that people let their fears surrounding possible retribution, anger from people affected, or concerns about the arduous effort it takes to work through any documentation process stop them from removing people from key work processes or positions. Because these fears are so strong, people stay in positions that are not right for them, the other people in the group suffer, and trust erodes.

People also use excuses to explain or validate why they will continue to put up with someone who is a chronic underperformer. You may hear comments such as "They have been here for so long" or "They are two years from retirement." Given systems thinking, there are always impacts to the larger group when you protect one person at the expense of the whole. Are good employees leaving? Is your group performance substandard? Are any of these tensions affecting morale? If your answers are yes, then make a different choice. There are many possibilities to managing the situation.

Strategies to Move Forward with the Trust Repair Model without Others

If you have made the decision to stop wasting energy, or if you cannot repair trust with the person or group, you can work through the Trust Repair Model by yourself. It is always more effective to do it with all the affected people, but sometimes that is just not possible. The table below illustrates some strategies for you to consider if you need relief and want to move forward.

Phase	Individual trust repair strategies
Reflect	The Reflect phase is always about you, and the tools and strategies presented in this book should all be applicable to helping you.
Understand	If you cannot speak to the person directly: • Speak with a trusted confidant and ask the person to serve as a sounding board and provide another perspective to consider as you sort through what happened.
	• Assess the violation of trust situation, acknowledge your part, and apologize. This is an important act that will help you with closure and release any ongoing energy caused by the situation remaining unresolved. You need to acknowledge it even if the other person is unwilling to hear it. You can acknowledge and apologize quietly in your head, write it down and send a letter, or if that is not possible, use your trusted confidant to express your sentiments.

Phase	Individual trust repair strategies
Repair	Repair is most difficult when the other party does not want to work through it with you. • Write a letter to the person; it is your choice whether to mail it. Write your story of the impact of the trust violation: your intentions, your sense of what the other person experienced, and whatever else you want to explain. Acknowledge your part, apologize, and write about how you intend to move forward and your wishes for the other person to move forward. • If the violation of trust was an ignorance issue (e.g., "I didn't know"), demonstrate what you have learned. In the future you can demonstrate, through your actions, that you have corrected the problem. The person may or may not notice, but you will know, and that helps you move forward. • If the violation of trust was an integrity issue (e.g., "I served my own interests at the expense of others"), you will need to publicly acknowledge and apologize in person or in writing. The person may or may not respond. Remember, it takes several instances of demonstrating your integrity behavioral adjustments to make up for the violation if you did it.

Phase	Individual trust repair strategies
Evolve	Adopt principles that move you forward, such as: • I will release myself from being held hostage, because there are actions that I can own and make a difference in my environment. • I will honor that other people have different ways of processing; they may not be ready to work through the issues yet. • I will not let someone else's delay in working through the trust repair process delay my ability to work through it. • I will be mindful of my intentions and my impact on others. • I will forgive myself and the other person. • I will remember that I always have options and can make choices that work for me.

What If People Simply Hate Each Other?

Working with people who loathe each other is problematic because it affects everyone in the group. In a *Harvard Business Review* article, Liane Davey offered some sage advice:

1. "Before addressing the interpersonal tension between people, it is important to ensure the conflict isn't stemming from more systemic issues. Do people have clarity about roles, expectations, and a set of measures that promote collaboration rather than competition? Make sure the relationship is set up for success."[1]

2. Consider your own frustration with the people and reflect on any judgments you have about them. "If you are fed up and unwilling to be empathetic, you won't be in a position to help. Hatred is the product of miscommunication, misunderstanding, and fear—empathy can dissolve it."[2] You

must begin with a mindset that these people are capable of rebuilding their relationship. Pay attention to your own emotional reactions (emotional intelligence). Davey suggests that you "compose yourself or risk provoking more anxiety in the people you are trying to calm down."

3. Provide timely feedback to people whenever you observe poor interactions. "Jacki, I notice that whenever Shelley is speaking, you stand up and start walking around the room. I'm curious why you do this when she speaks?" At this point, it is important to get sound and current information from Jacki and test whether your observation of her disrespect for Shelley is at play. The key is to get to the root causes and, once exposed, help people craft new working relationships.

4. Encourage both parties to consider other possibilities about each other. Perhaps they need some support to have a conversation together, such as a neutral facilitator or mediation.

If people remain unwilling to move from a position of hate, anger, hurt, or frustration, you still get to make a choice about what you intend to do. You can find ways to function that work for you and allow you to stay, or you can remove yourself from this group. Anything is possible; you do not have to stay stuck.

Special Circumstances

There are some categories of people whom I did not study that affect the repair process of trust in groups. People who have mental illness, developmental disabilities, or delays need special consideration from their groups when working through the repair of trust. For example, people with social disabilities who have high anxiety or people on the autism spectrum may find that participating in activities that

People with varying disabilities know what they need, so instead of guessing, please ask them.

require a lot of social interaction will not necessarily tap into their important input, and it is extremely difficult for them.

My suggestion is to first ask them what is needed so that they feel comfortable with talking about and exploring the issues. People with varying disabilities know what they need, so instead of guessing, please ask them. You might find that one of the reasons trust repair activities have not worked yet is because their disability has not been fully considered in the design of your activities. There are multiple ways to provide input to group processes that do not have to amplify the disability. It is always important to play to the strengths of people. Leaders must be sensitive and able to appropriately access all feedback and contributions. Additionally, check in with your human resource professionals for guidance on working with people with disabilities.

Summary

Sometimes you find yourself in a situation where people do not want to repair trust or are unable to repair trust, and you must make some choices. You can move forward with the Trust Repair Model and not remain stuck. If you find yourself stuck in the wasted energy cycle, where you keep trying to make others change or try to improve the situation yourself, it will drain and frustrate you. To get out of this unhealthy cycle, reflect on what happened, acknowledge your part, apologize, forgive yourself, and stop wasting energy trying to change others who do not want to change.

To be fair in your attempts to repair trust, be conscious and adjust your strategies for people who have disabilities that affect their ability to fully participate. There are also people who simply do not get along or who cannot perform the requirements of the job. Leaders must learn how to support and develop people but also know when to make changes to best suit the person and the group. In the end, staying stuck is a choice.

CHAPTER 10

Tools

It ought to be remembered that there is nothing more difficult to take in hand, more perilous to conduct, or more uncertain in its success, than to take the lead in the introduction of a new order of things.
—Niccolò Machiavelli

I designed and prepared this practical chapter to support your growth and equip you with tools to repair trust and strengthen relationships in groups. I begin with sharing pitfalls normally encountered in this process and ideas on what to do about it. Then, I provide descriptions on how to use tools to support each phase of the Trust Repair Model. These tools do not represent the entirety of options available to address your trust issues nor are they guaranteed to always prove successful; however, I have used each and every one of the tools I share with you and have found success using them. I wish you the best as you move forward with the important work of repairing trust and strengthening relationships. You can do it!

Pitfalls to Avoid and Suggestions to Remedy Them in Repairing Trust in Groups

Pitfall: Believing That Training Fixes Everything or Is the First Step in Repairing Trust in Groups

Training tends to be aimed at team building because people are experiencing unhealthy interpersonal dynamics (e.g., rude behavior, disengagement). If you target training at that level, you may not be getting to the root issues. Trust repair takes more than one workshop. Go back up the Trust Behaviors Framework, start at the top, and reflect on the potential sources of trust erosion.

Pitfall: Thinking You Have All the Information regarding the Violations of Trust

How do you know if you have sound and current information regarding the situation? Are you acting on limited or fragmented information? You must be fair and get all the information from others involved. People experience what I call the first story syndrome: the first person to explain their side of what happened now becomes the filter that you use to listen and explore other sides of the story from other people involved. The first story is powerful because people are compelling, and you will have a tendency to develop empathy toward their side. You will need to be conscious about remaining neutral, empathetic, and curious as you listen to the other sides.

Pitfall: Permitting the Phrase "I'm Just Being Honest" to Allow Bullying or Unkind Behavior

Insist on creating and following feedback rules, ground rules, or other rules of engagement. There are professional, direct, and kind ways to give feedback. You will be perpetuating unhealthy interpersonal behaviors if bullying is allowed. Also check in and ask what the intention is behind the honest feedback and whether it is based upon sound and current information. You do not want to spread rumors, either.

Pitfall: Permitting Righteousness and Ego Issues to Get in the Way

Everyone makes mistakes; own it. If you think you are above the fray, you are contributing to the conditions where people are fearful and hide anything that is not perfect. People are human beings who make mistakes, say the wrong things, and react too quickly when they should have reflected first. Do not let ego and righteousness get in the way of acknowledging your part. Embody humility.

Pitfall: Holding on to Hurt and Casting It into Every Future Interaction

It does not serve you or the group to hold on to hurt for a long time. It affects your personal and professional well-being, and it affects the group. Projecting your hurt into future interactions only compounds the problem, and past problems do not necessarily relate to other situations. Work through the trust repair model and learn how to resolve the painful issues so that they do not seep into other areas.

Pitfall: Thinking There Is Only One Way to Handle Trust Issues

Good improvisation or jazz musicians know how to adjust their part to whatever is happening. When you work with the unique dynamics of people in groups, do your part well, listen, and adjust as needed. There are many ways to handle trust issues, and you may have to try several to make a difference.

Pitfall: Giving Up Too Early or Not Giving Enough Time to Repairing Trust

Give yourself the gift of time: build in time to reflect and design thoughtful responses to trust issues. In my trust repair study, it took an average of six to thirty-six months and several activities to repair trust and strengthen relationships in groups. Giving up after one or two attempts at activities aimed to support trust because the group is not "there" yet does not mean your attempts are not working. Do not give up too early!

Pitfall: Being Closed-Minded about Other Perspectives

Stay open and curious and explore other perspectives, because yours is not the only one. Consider the metaphor of a theater performance where everyone has a different experience. The actors on the stage have individual and shared experiences. How does it look from the orchestra pit? What about the guests in the balcony? What about the stage, sound, and lighting crew? You must remain open to listening and consciously seek out other perspectives. Your take on the situation is never fully complete without viewpoints from other people.

Tools to Support the Reflect Phase

Spending time reflecting is as important as drawing up blueprints for a building. You would not just show up at a job site and throw materials together. Essentially, this is what you would do if you fail to reflect on the situation, instead of moving forward with attempts to fix it.

To further assist you in the first stage of the trust repair process (Reflect), you may use the following tools by yourself or with a group:

- Reflection Questions
- Trust Assessment
- Choice Matrix

Tool: Reflection Questions

Purpose

To provide questions that explore the trust violation and your experience. These questions will help you sort through your initial reaction and do some deep thinking about the impact. You should have a better idea of your next steps after answering these questions.

How to Use

- **Individuals:** Reflect on the questions personally and make notes. It may take one to two hours to complete.

- **Groups:** Share the questions and invite each person to reflect on their own. Because of the way the questions are framed, it is an individual exercise. Wait to foster group conversations until the Understand phase.

Questions

What happened? Briefly describe the situation.

What am I feeling?

Interview the feelings: Where did they come from? How strong are they?

Am I feeling emotionally triggered?

What bothers me the most about what happened?

Is this my issue, or do I need to work it out with others? Do I still need to interact and work with these people in an ongoing relationship?

What was my role and contribution to the current situation? Am I open to exploring my personal liability (accepting fault)?

What are others' roles and contributions to the current situation? List and describe. Consider the bigger picture.

What present conditions are fueling the situation from the group or the larger organization/community?

What is the nature of the trust violation itself?

Competence: Did the person have the appropriate knowledge, skills, or abilities?

Integrity: How did the person's behaviors, character, or choices impact me and others?

Would I characterize it as accidental, opportunistic, or intentional?

How clear am I about what happened and why?

Is my information sound and current, or am I operating from old experiences?

What assumptions am I making?

What other perspectives could tell a different story?

Are there other possible reasons for this to be happening?

If I move forward with the trust repair process, what are my goals and intentions? What do I want?

What do I anticipate being the most challenging to me and why?

What do I need to learn more about? How will I do that?

What is the cost of the current situation?

What is the cost of doing nothing?

What is at stake in moving forward with trust repair for me and the group?

What support do I need to move forward?

Tool in Action: Reflection Questions

I worked for a small organization that was a member of a large network. As part of an agreement to share resources, I facilitated the creation of a process improvement training program with another company that would benefit both organizations. I had a lot to offer since I had worked in the process improvement field for twenty years. Yet my facilitation style is one where I work to leverage and capitalize on everyone's talents in the group, not just demonstrate how much I know about process improvement.

As we worked on a model that would serve both organizations, we agreed that we would put some of the pieces into practice early. Team members agreed to take a piece of our curriculum and try it out in their sections, and then I would check in with them in between our monthly team meetings. I had good success connecting with all but one team member, Donovan. I reached out to him several times via email, voice mail, and texts. He was slow to reply, and when I did connect with him, he was superficial and did not always complete the assignment. Donovan worked for another company in the network. His nonresponsiveness continued for several months. When he attended our team meetings, he avoided me. When team members discussed their appreciation for practicing the elements of our leadership development program and conversing with me during our check-ins, Donovan stated that he did not find value in the check-in connections.

That statement from Donovan triggered an emotional reaction within me. However, I stayed neutral on the outside because I was genuinely interested in understanding why. I asked him separately, outside of the group, in my effort to stay curious, and he gave a nonanswer: "I know what to do and don't find this a good use of my time to practice this stuff in between meetings." He also shared details about how he operates: "When I meet someone, I can assess in the first few minutes whether it is someone I want to work with or need anything from." That was it. In my mind, he had written me off as inconsequential and not useful, and he did not want to work with me. I was offended.

I had a choice to make. Over the ensuing months, these interactions with him, his nonresponsiveness, and frankly his shortsightedness in failing to understand that people are more complex than to be written off within five minutes made me lose trust in him. I also lost trust because he didn't have credibility in this field, even though he thought he "got it intuitively." So, I had a choice to give him feedback, make adjustments, or let it go.

After contemplating the reflection questions above, I made a conscious choice about not giving feedback to Donovan. Why? My ego had been assaulted for sure. I felt disrespected and wanted him to know that I knew he had written me off. But then, how do I really know? I never directly asked him. I just believed in my whole being that he did. I also knew he was busy, but that's an excuse for not stepping up and doing his part of the work in between meetings. The real question for me was, What would I gain by having a feedback conversation with him? What was my motive? My initial motive was not so positive. I wanted to pick at his ego and dive deeply into his understanding of process management, because I wasn't seeing or experiencing it. I could have used my expertise to stump and humiliate him. Instead, I gave myself the gift of time and waited until I had a clear head and my emotions subsided. In the end, because we only had one more team meeting and he worked for another company in the network, I chose not to devote additional time and energy to Donovan. I chose to focus my attention on the rest of the team, and we created an incredible program that is still in use after six years.

In my reflection, it was clear I had an emotional trigger and a story around that. I interviewed my feelings and understood my reaction. I very much want to be respected for knowledge and skills I bring to the table and to be respected for my humility. In particular, though I have a great deal of expertise, I also consider myself a continuous learner. I get annoyed with people who act like know-it-alls. Donovan's actions got under my skin. When he appeared to not respect my expertise by writing me off, it was a double whammy.

In the end, I chose to honor and live my core values. After completing my inner reflective work, I realized that only my ego would have had something to prove (e.g., that I had expertise). I also reframed his behavior from an emotional trigger to one that reminded me that not everyone can see how their actions impact others. He may continue to believe that I did not add value; I cannot let that overly influence my own beliefs about my value.

Not every disrespecting action requires a response; you can reframe it as an invitation to reflect and deepen understanding about yourself.

Tool: Trust Assessment

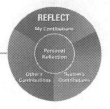

Purpose

To assess the current situation and provide a suggested response for next steps.

How to Use

- **Individuals:** Read the assessment, select a number response, and tally the score. Read the suggested course of action at the bottom.

- **Groups:** Give the assessment to members of the group. They can use it individually or turn in the responses (anonymously if desired) and let a neutral person compile the data. Present the data back to the group. Discuss.

It may be important to clarify the trust situation so group members understand if there is one incident to consider while responding to these questions or whether it is the general climate of trust within the group.

Assessment

Reflect on a current trust situation. Determine whether it is one situation or the general climate of trust within the group that you are assessing. Answer the questions by selecting a number that best fits the intensity. Tally your score and refer to the corresponding suggested course of action at the bottom.

Trust Situation: _____

1. Personal impact: I have been personally impacted by the trust situation.
   (Not affected)   1   2   3   4   5   (Significantly affected)

2. Importance: It is important for me to repair trust and resolve the situation with this group/person.
   (Unimportant)   1   2   3   4   5   (Extremely important)

3. Emotional triggers: The situation triggered an emotional reaction within me.
   (Did not bother me)   1   2   3   4   5   (Enormously upset)

4. Resolution: I believe this situation will not resolve itself without doing something directly about it.
   (Already resolved)   1   2   3   4   5   (Needs help to resolve)

5. Involvement: This situation involves others beyond just me.
   (Only affects me)   1   2   3   4   5   (Affects others)

6. Repeatability: If unresolved, I believe the situation will be repeated.
   (Won't happen again)   1   2   3   4   5   (High repeat probability)

7. Roles: This situation has affected people's roles and responsibilities.
   (Roles unaffected)   1   2   3   4   5   Roles affected, altered)

8. Core processes: The situation has impaired our core work processes.
   (Workflow unchanged)   1   2   3   4   5   (Huge disruption in workflow)

9. Communication: Communication patterns are disrupted and unhealthy.
   (Healthy)   1   2   3   4   5   (Disrupted and unhealthy)

10. Interpersonal dynamics: Group members are treating each other terribly.
    (Dynamics are fine)   1   2   3   4   5   (Dynamics are terrible)

11. Willingness: I am willing to work on improving the situation.
    (Not willing)   1   2   3   4   5   (Very willing)

12. Risk: If unresolved, I believe there is significant risk to people, our organization, or our customers.
    (Little risk)   1   2   3   4   5   (Significant risk)

Tally: _____

Low = 12–28 points

Moderate = 29–45 points

High = 46–60 points

What Your Score Might Suggest

Low: It appears the violations of trust are not at the level that you believe you need to take action with other people to resolve. Be mindful that you may need to pay attention to the impact the situation has on others and be ready engage in dialogue even if you do not see the immediate need. The situation may not affect you as much as it might others. Try to find any lessons in the situation and consciously work to improve relationships.

Moderate: The violations of trust are at a level where you notice the disruption of work, communication, and other dynamics in the group, but things are probably still functional even if they are not operating optimally. A moderate level warrants attention and work. Include trust repair activities and discussions in staff meetings and make conscious choices about getting to the root cause of the problems; otherwise, it could worsen.

High: A high score is a strong signal that your group needs immediate support to repair violations of trust. Groups cannot sustain healthy operations when people cannot talk together, trust each other, or work efficiently. Check out the tools and suggestions in the Trust Repair Model. You might need some support from people who have the skills to help your group get unstuck.

| Tool: Choice Matrix

Purpose

The Choice Matrix increases awareness of choices and the ability to act intentionally.[1] This tool helps when people feel stuck or victimized and believe they have no power to change a situation. It is also used to help identify underlying belief systems that may be preventing people from moving forward.

How to Use

- **Individuals:** Look at the four quadrants and consider the choices and what is influencing the situation. Remind yourself and others that you always have a choice, even if you think you do not. You have the power to influence the current situation or at least shift your thinking about it so you are in a healthier place. The key will be to help uncover underlying beliefs that are keeping you stuck or believing you have no power to change.

- **Groups:** Explain the quadrants and meanings. Share stories or examples of each choice. Ask group members to first reflect individually their own personal and professional examples of the four choice quadrants. Break into groups of two to four people and invite them to discuss examples and listen for patterns. Ask small groups to summarize learning and share with the larger group. Discuss. Then, as a whole group, ask how the group makes choices and what patterns are present in the group. Are they effective? What adjustments should the group consider to be more aware of choices? Discuss.

The Matrix

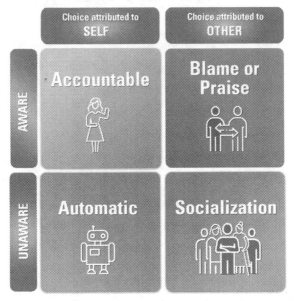

Choice Awareness Matrix

	Choice attributed to SELF	Choice attributed to OTHER
AWARE	Accountable	Blame or Praise
UNAWARE	Automatic	Socialization

Source: Edith Whitfield Seashore. Used with permission.

Steps

1. Understand the quadrant layout: The columns are choices that you attribute to yourself and choices you attribute to others. Rows are choices you make that you are either aware or unaware of.

2. **Accountable:** When you are aware that you are in control of your choices, you are accountable for what you choose. You make the choice to work where you do, to volunteer where you want, and whether to accept social invitations. You are fully aware of your decisions and have power over your choices. You own your mistakes and shortcomings, rather than blame others or make excuses. You are accountable for your choices.

3. **Blame or praise:** When you are aware of the choices but give control of your choices to others, you can blame or praise them. People in this category claim that others "make" them do things, or they feel like they have no choice and must go along. The question becomes, do you see yourself as a victim? If you do, you are giving your power of choice away to others. This quadrant is an energy-draining space because you believe the power to make the choice is out of your control. Examples include:

    a. Feeling taken advantage of when team members ask you to constantly take notes at the meeting when there are other people who could do it. You begrudgingly type up the notes. You are aware that you are doing it even though you do not want to, but you believe you have no choice but to type the notes. You can blame others when you do not get your other work done and you are the victim here.

    b. There is plenty of blame and victim mentality in workplaces. Statements such as:

        *   *My boss* is terrible and never shares any information with us, so we never know what is going on.
        *   *They* will not let us do anything about these cumbersome procedures, so I hate my work.
        *   *They* handled the customer crisis terribly, and now we have to clean it up.
        *   *I have to* go early and set up because no one else will.
        *   *I have to* double check other's work because they make mistakes.

    c. You can also give your power away by overpraising others. For example, a work colleague sees that you have the talent to take on a big project and encourages you to do so. You complete the project, and at the end, when the boss recognizes you, you give all the credit to the colleague who encouraged you in the first place. Acknowledging their encouragement is great, but over-praising the other person and not taking credit for the work you actually did keeps you in this category too by attributing your choice to others.

d. The key with the blame or praise quadrant is that we all fit into it at times. Remember, it is an energy-draining and powerless space because you have given your choice to others. Become aware that you are here by listening to your own language: if you say, "I have to," most likely you are in victim mode. How does it feel if you changed your language to "I choose"? Can you think of other choices that work better for you? How can you own part of the situation? Using the words "I choose to type up the notes" gives you your power back. That may stimulate you to say, "I choose to type the notes up today, and then it is up to another member of the team to do it next time."

4. **Automatic:** When you behave in a way that is routine and reactive, and you are unaware of the choices you are making, you do it automatically or by habit. Being on automatic gives you the illusion that you do not have a choice. Examples include:

a. Saying yes or no quickly without thinking about it first. Too quick to offer help? Say you will do everything and it is no problem? You are most likely on automatic. Maybe it is a problem, and you do not have time to assemble the report, take the kids to the dentist, or add one more project to your plate. But if you say yes without thinking, you are in this quadrant. Remember that you have a choice, and it is important to be intentional about it by increasing your awareness that you are doing it.

b. From a leadership perspective, you might be contributing to the problems of other people. There are yes people; these are your go-to folks whom you can rely on to do things in a crunch or you know the quality of their work so you continually go to them. This is where problems arise. Are you overloading these people? When you are unaware and on automatic, there is an impact on other team members who see you constantly go to the same person when some of them would welcome the opportunity for an assignment.

c. Your core beliefs fuel your automatic choices. For example, if you grew up in a family that expressed beliefs like "Asking for help means weakness," you may make choices about trying to do everything yourself because you think that you do not need outside help. You do not question this because you are unaware that you keep doing it, because it is what is natural to you.

d. Core beliefs in work settings usually include views about how groups operate and how work gets done. These beliefs could be "taking turns is important, so everyone should have to take meeting notes on a rotational basis," or "ensure equal speaking time among all members regardless of rank or seniority." However, what if other people in the group have different core beliefs about how work gets done or how the group should operate? This is a big area for stress in teams. You might have a core belief that people should always come to meetings prepared, and others may have beliefs that it is okay to take the time needed to do quality work. At a basic level, both are good beliefs. Yet both can cause tension in the team when people get annoyed with each other when their behaviors, based on their core beliefs, conflict.

e. There are other beliefs that fuel your automatic responses to the choices you make, such as "I don't have a college degree, so I can't apply for that job." With an underlying belief like that, you are making a choice to not apply for jobs that you might be the perfect fit for because of what you are saying to your inner self. Other beliefs could be:

- Only supervisors assign work.
- You must go through the hierarchy before you talk to another group.
- Wait to be told what to do.
- The coach/leader/supervisor is always right.

How are these beliefs serving you? Are they helpful or harmful? When you are on automatic, you are not thinking; you are just doing. Raise your awareness that your belief system is influencing your choices and then become intentional about what choice you want to make.

5. **Socialization:** When you are unaware of your choices about what to do or not do, what you consider okay, or what may be right or wrong, when these have been heavily influenced by others' core beliefs, you are acting from socialization. Socialization occurs in workplaces, families, sport teams, and more broadly, society. Human beings are wired to be in connection with others. We pay attention to what is happening and, in general, want to be accepted and included. To do this, we are socialized about what it means to be a part of the group. Socialization influences the choices that we

may not even be aware we are making because it is just the way it is and is reinforced by others in the group. Examples include:

a. Belief systems within organizations are socialized and part of the culture. In some organizations, there is a strong belief that someone must have direct experience or education to be able to effectively lead others in that field. When hiring a person to lead a division of engineers, do you set aside great candidates just because they do not have an engineering degree? If you do, this may be an indicator of a socialized belief. Why not find a spectacular leader who can actually let the engineers do their part well and let the leader do their part well? If you are unaware that you are making choices to only consider and hire people with certain backgrounds based on a socialized belief, you may be missing out on hiring some incredible people.

b. Think about how you grew up and what rules there were about how you treated guests in your home. Your parents or guardians created the dos and don'ts of hospitality and could reinforce it with just a raise of their eyebrows. There are also rules about how you were expected to act when you were a guest in other homes. Choices about whether you could ask for a second helping of food, whether you had to clean up after yourself and strip the bed in the morning, whether you were expected to get up before others or stay on the same sleep schedule are all examples of socialization.

c. In different parts of world or within your community, people have been socialized to treat others in certain ways. I have a friend who explained her "phone voice." Growing up in the southern part of the United States, no matter how she was feeling at the time, there was an expected way of answering the phone or greeting people with the tone of her voice, her word choices, and, if in person, the smile on her face. She also shared many other expectations about what it meant to be a young southern woman and how it influences her choices.

d. Socialization feeds stereotypes and, if left unchecked, limits choices and could actually cause harm to people. For example, in meetings, are women expected to take notes? Do men have to open doors and yield entry to others first? Do young people have to sit in silence and wait to be invited to speak?

e. Families influence choices of their individual members through socialization as well. For example, "We handle things in the family" or "Don't share our dirty laundry with others"—these expectations influence your choice about whether you disclose anything to others or whether you keep information to yourself. Does this belief limit the choice about seeking the help of a counselor if needed?

Not all socialization is bad. People are generally unaware of the choices that they are making that are heavily influenced by others. The key is to become aware and then make choices that move you toward accountability. Remind yourself and your team members that you have choices on how to respond.

Source: Edith Seashore for the Choice Matrix. Used with permission. Descriptions by Wendy Fraser

Tool in Action: Choice Matrix

Choice Awareness Matrix

I attended a weekend workshop in my graduate program where every student had to prepare a case study to present to the group. As we were getting ready to start, I offered to take notes for the first person who presented their case. I figured that it would be helpful to that person to receive the highlights of the questions and comments from the group. In my mind, I figured I would start and others would volunteer so that we all would take turns. While I was accountable and clear about my choice to volunteer, I was unaware that what fueled my choice was a belief that I have about the way groups work. In my mind, good group members take turns, so I offered to take notes to demonstrate with the expectation that others would follow.

The second student got up to start their case study and asked me if I would take notes for them. In a split second, and without thinking, I said yes. Saying yes too quickly usually means I am on automatic. So, I took notes. When the third person got up to start their case and barely asked me to take notes again by sort of nodding in my direction, I was now astonished and incensed inside. In my head, I was saying all sorts of things: "I'm not everyone's secretary. Why don't others volunteer? I'm feeling taken advantage of. Don't others know they need to do their part and take turns?" Of course, this was all going on inside me, and I was gracious and polite on the outside while fuming with indignation on the inside.

Noticing all of this was Charlie Seashore, who was leading the workshop with his partner and wife, Edie Seashore. Speaking with Charlie alone, I shared my disappointment that others had not stepped up to take notes. He told me that I had made the whole thing happen by first operating from my automatic belief system about the way I thought groups should work. "Did you ask anyone else how they wanted the note taking to go?" I had not. It was a huge discovery to me to understand that my view of the world was different from that of the other people there. I needed to make my hopes for turn taking more explicit and discuss it with my fellow students rather than operate on my own assumptions. As a group, we needed to discuss and make agreements together, rather than me thinking about what we should do and then getting all upset when it didn't happen. They were not accountable to my rules.

Next, Charlie reminded me that when I became aware that others were not following my lead, when the third person got up, that I had a choice then, too. Instead, I wasted energy and fumed inside, blaming others for not volunteering and becoming a victim by feeling taken advantage of. Once I became aware that I was operating on my own automatic belief system, I could have stopped things and asked for someone else to take notes.

The gift of Edie's Choice Matrix tool is to remind you and your team that you always have choices, even if it feels like you do not. Work to become more conscious and aware of your choices so that it works for you. Keep the Choice Matrix tool present in your meetings with group members, keep a copy of the tool on your wall or near your workstation, and simply remind yourself often "What choice do I have?" Edie was my dearest mentor, and I can still hear her voice when I feel most stuck: "Can you think of another choice?" Yes, I can...and you can, too!

Tools to Support the Understand Phase

After you have reflected and decided to move forward with repairing trust and strengthening relationships, you will need to work with the people involved to understand what happened to contribute to the current situation.

The next several pages have tools that can assist you in the second stage of the trust repair process: Understand. You can use these tools and activities by yourself or use them with a group.

- Ladder of Inference
- Mediation
- Video and Discussion: "On Being Wrong"

Tool: Ladder of Inference

Purpose

The Ladder of Inference illustrates the evaluation and judgment process people use to make meaning of situations and take actions.[2] The ladder serves as a metaphor for our line of thinking from the moment we take in information, evaluate it, and move to decision-making. This process often goes unnoticed and can get us into trouble if we make assumptions based on incomplete information or biases.

Ladder of Inference

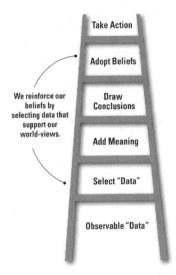

Adapted from C. Argryis, Overcoming Organizational Defenses: Facilitating Organizational Learning, *1ˢᵗ ed., 1990. Permission granted by Pearson Education, Inc., Upper Saddle River, New Jersey. Material includes concepts from "Ladder of Inference from Peter M. Senge, Art Kleiner, Charlotte Roberts, C., Richard, B. Ross, and Bryan J. Smith,* The Fifth Discipline Fieldbook: Strategies and Tools for Building a Learning Organization, *1994. Used by permission of Doubleday, an imprint of the Knopf Doubleday Publishing Group, a division of Penguin Random House LLC. All rights reserved.*

How to Use

- **Individuals:** Start at the bottom, work up to the top, and review the ladder descriptions of each rung. Reflect on the reinforcing reality between the facts selected and beliefs people hold. Think about a few instances when you were at the top of your ladder. Why? What contributed to it? Compare that to when you have been in the middle of the ladder. What circumstances contributed to you being in the midpoint? What are you learning about your patterns? Remember, you can always ask yourself "why" questions and remind yourself to gather more data as a method to keep your assumptions in check.

- **Groups:** Explain the rungs and meanings. Share stories or examples of each rung. Ask group members to first reflect individually their own personal and professional examples of the ladder. Break into groups of two to four people and invite them to discuss examples and listen for patterns. Ask the small groups to summarize learning and share with the larger group. Discuss. Then as a whole group, ask how the group makes decisions and what patterns are present in the group when selecting data, adding meaning, and creating conclusions. Are they effective? What adjustments should the group consider to be more aware of their beliefs and what data they select? Discuss.

The key takeaway is to facilitate a discussion where people realize how each person goes up and down the ladder in different circumstances. Everyone can support healthy discussions and decision-making if they continue to ask questions about the data selected, meanings added, assumptions made, and beliefs that support the decisions.

Steps

1. Describe the rungs of the ladder and provide examples.

    a. Start at the bottom of the ladder where there is simply **observable data**.

    Think about how a recording device might record everything: this is the observable data. Observable data for a group of people who are at a meeting are the actual words, gestures, tone of voice, timing and cadence of expressions, seating arrangements, documents used and unused, written notes or symbols on display screens, logged discussion notes, questions, who gets called upon to speak and who does not, etc.

    b. Next, people naturally **select data** to pay attention to.

    Both consciously and unconsciously, people pick things out of experiences, conversations, written communication, interactions with others, and observations.

    c. People then **add meaning** to their selected data, again without thinking much about it.

    They add cultural and personal meaning to these things as a way of situating the information within their thinking processes. Meaning can come from a person's upbringing, cultural influences, past experiences, professional standards, education, core values, and so on.

    d. After determining meaning, and often without thinking, people **draw conclusions**.

    The path between adding meaning and drawing conclusions is typically very fast. This is where people are quick to jump to conclusions by taking one gesture, word, or action and instantly determining what it means.

e. People then **adopt beliefs** based on these conclusions.

People form beliefs and hold on to them based on their experiences and what they know to be true (to them). Beliefs get reinforced when people select certain data that reinforce their reality. Beliefs are hard to shift because they are deeply rooted in people's lived experiences, values, and the meaning they have put into their selected data. When people are on this rung of the ladder, it is more difficult to help them see other possible meanings or conclusions of what the data says.

f. Finally, when people are at the top rung of the ladder, they **take action**.

These actions are justified in their minds because they are based on their beliefs, and those come from their selected data, so to them, they are based in evidence and truth.

2. Share the reinforcing belief systems that keep people stuck. Show the model arrows between the rungs that select data and adopt beliefs.

Our beliefs have a big effect on what data we select and can lead us to ignore other facts altogether. People will select certain data that reinforce their beliefs. For example, if I believe that another person dislikes me, in every interaction I will both consciously and unconsciously look for gestures, words, or other things that reinforce this belief. I may see that the other person looked away from me when I was speaking. I can use this as fuel to my belief that they do not like me. However, what if the other person was just glancing at a poster on the wall? The fact that the other person looked away may have nothing to do with me. But, I select that piece of data and jump to the top of my ladder by reinforcing my belief.

3. Describe the benefits of using the Ladder of Inference.

   The greatest benefit of knowing about the Ladder of Inference is to bring into our awareness our thinking and judgment processes. It can help people think about how they select data, add meaning, draw conclusions, and then move to judgment and action. The ladder helps people avoid living in their own assumption-land.

4. Illustrate the uses of the ladder in conversations.

   The ladder can be used to help people move down the rungs by helping them to become curious about their line of thinking and reasoning. Using what I fondly call the two-year-old technique, asking "why" questions is enormously helpful. This also aligns with the Five Whys tool in Lean Six Sigma thinking. Being curious about the data that was originally selected, and how the person added meaning to it will enable you to discover more about the person's thinking process, but it can allow you to add additional data as well. For example, you could offer that you were at the same meeting and when you heard the discussion you saw things differently. Sharing your data and the meaning you added will broaden the thinking field for the other person. Hosting these kinds of conversations underscores the power of the Ladder of Inference.

5. Remind people that the use of absolute language is an indicator that a person is at the top of the ladder.

   People at the top of the ladder live in absolutes: "She *always* says that," "He *never* follows through," and so on. Realistically, it is impossible to have anyone always or never do anything. If people are using absolute language, that is a clue that they are near or at the top of the ladder. You must help them see other possible meanings the data could have or select more data to consider.

6. Illustrate the uses of the ladder in individual reflection.

The ladder can support individual reflection by inviting people to stop and interview beliefs and actions. *Why am I thinking this? Why is the other person doing that? Where did this thinking come from? When did I first start thinking this way? What beliefs are informing my decisions? What other options are there? What other ways can I derive meaning from the data I selected? What sound and current data do I have that supports this thinking? Are there other ways to consider what is happening? What other data is out there?* In this reflection, also consider if, under certain circumstances, you skip rungs in the ladder. Why does this happen? What assumptions are you making? How can you stop or slow down your thought processes and consider a wider array of data and possible meaning?

7. Host a team discussion.

The ladder is an excellent team tool that opens up the ability to check in with each other about assumptions and make the reasoning process more transparent. When a group learns this tool together, they learn a common language and a model that will help them challenge each other's thinking and be curious while reducing the personal worry about offending someone.

Ladder of Inference

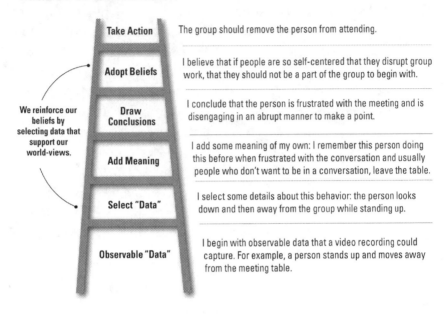

	Take Action	The group should remove the person from attending.
	Adopt Beliefs	I believe that if people are so self-centered that they disrupt group work, that they should not be a part of the group to begin with.
We reinforce our beliefs by selecting data that support our world-views.	**Draw Conclusions**	I conclude that the person is frustrated with the meeting and is disengaging in an abrupt manner to make a point.
	Add Meaning	I add some meaning of my own: I remember this person doing this before when frustrated with the conversation and usually people who don't want to be in a conversation, leave the table.
	Select "Data"	I select some details about this behavior: the person looks down and then away from the group while standing up.
	Observable "Data"	I begin with observable data that a video recording could capture. For example, a person stands up and moves away from the meeting table.

Questions to Help Get down the Ladder

Why did I/we think this way?

What data did I/we select and add meaning to? Was there other data to consider?

What meaning did I/we add to the data? What other interpretations are there?

What choices do I/we have about broadening beliefs and possibilities of other ways of gathering data and drawing conclusions?

Did I/we skip any rungs with this situation? Why?

Tool in Action: Ladder of Inference

Emotionally exhausted, Jenny was through with trying to fit into the team and decided to leave the organization. Unaware of her unhappiness and because of her desired skill set, organizational leaders asked if I could meet with Jenny to determine whether they could do anything to keep her.

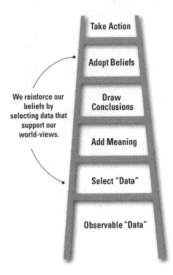

Ladder of Inference

I listened to Jenny explain her experiences and her decision to leave the team. Using the Ladder of Inference, Jenny was at the top rung: taking action. When we met, she was very clear that she wanted out of the situation. Informing this action was her belief that "no one respected" her. Knowing the way to move down the ladder is to ask questions, I asked her why she believed no one respected her. Jenny described interactions with fellow team members that left her feeling distraught, dismissed, and ignored. She concluded that if no one had time to talk with her or made weird faces when she tried to engage with them, they did not respect her as a colleague and did not care about what she had to offer.

Remember, when someone is in pain, do not judge or try to change their thinking or feeling about the situation. Remain open, curious, and inquire about the meaning the person puts into the experiences they are describing.

As we moved down the ladder in the conversation trying to explore the data selected and the meaning she put into it, Jenny shared that when she had ideas she wanted to talk with her colleagues about and walked into their offices, the nonverbal communication (slow to turn around to face her, wincing when she walked in—her selected data) made it clear to her that they did not want to talk with her or they really did not care much about her contributions (meaning added).

Next it was the rest of the team's turn to explore the situation and use the Ladder of Inference in a facilitated discussion. They heard firsthand her desire to leave because she felt disrespected and unwanted. Team members listened to Jenny's story uninterrupted and did a beautiful job of acknowledging her experience. One man began by expressing that he did not intend for her to feel hurt by his actions, but that he was a strong introvert and whenever she walked into his office unannounced or without knocking, he had to mentally disconnect from his work, turn his chair toward the door where she was standing, and then tune in to what she was saying. By that point, she was on her third or fourth sentence, and he would make grimacing faces trying to figure out what she was saying. By describing this, he provided new meaning to the data that Jenny selected. Another team member spoke up and expressed that she also was an introvert and whenever she was on her way to a meeting and Jenny would stop her in the hall, she would get distracted and would ask Jenny to talk later. This team member realized that her need to stay focused to prepare for her meeting could have been interpreted by Jenny that she was being dismissed, but that was not her intent (new conclusion).

The conversation turned to all team members describing how they operate best, and together they figured out some new ways to work with Jenny's extroverted needs to discuss things more spontaneously. For example, since all eight other members of her team were all self-described introverts, they asked Jenny if she could email them her questions or ideas in advance so they would have time to think about it, and when they met with her later, they could be fully engaged. They also discussed how to help keep the art of inquiry alive and reinforce a new team norm that they need to ask questions and check in on the meaning and conclusions people are generating so that they don't get to the top of the ladder. And yes, Jenny stayed with the team and the organization for several years.

Tool: Mediation

Purpose

When people are most stuck and need a safe, neutral process in which to discuss and resolve deep issues, mediation is a great process. Sometimes people reach an impasse or are unable able to sort through a situation so that they can listen to each other, understand what the other is trying to say, and resolve the issues. At its core, mediation is an intervention in a process or relationship dispute that helps people resolve differences, make new agreements, and move forward.

How to Use

- **Individuals:** Mediation is a process to help two or more people work through an issue where they are most stuck. Other than reviewing the process below to learn about it, mediation is not typically an individual tool.

- **Groups:** Use a neutral mediator trained in conflict resolution to help people communicate with each other, present their perspectives, identify the issues that need to be resolved, develop options for resolving those issues, and work out an agreement that the people involved believe is fair and reasonable. The process is best used with two people who need support in their discussions. Occasionally, three or four people may need to participate in the mediation process. Consider whether it makes sense to begin with pairs and then move to the larger group if there are other unresolved issues. The whole idea of mediation is to provide a private, small, neutral setting for discussion. However, if there is a group of five or more who need support having deeper discussions, mediation is not the right tool. It becomes more group facilitation rather than mediation.

Steps

1. Mediation should be an invitation to the people who need to resolve trust issues or work through differences that are keeping them stuck. The process will not be effective if anyone was told to be there. The decision to participate must be of their own free will.

2. People need to be willing to listen to each other and be ready to make adjustments to move forward. They cannot come in wanting to make the other side change. Each person must be willing to make adjustments themselves.

3. Find a neutral setting, preferably outside of the normal work setting, to invite a fresh mindset. People tend to hold on to the same rationale and mindsets if the mediated conversation is held in the same place where people are getting most stuck. Human beings are creatures of habit; a new and neutral location will affect communication patterns.

4. Review and agree on mediation ground rules.
    *   No interruptions during each person's opportunity to tell their story.
    *   Respectful listening and mindful nonverbal behaviors are expected (e.g., no eye rolling or heavy sighs that indicate disagreement).
    *   This is a confidential process; the only expressed words leaving the mediation session will be the ones agreed to by the people involved. The mediator is a neutral party and will not disclose anything to anyone, or the process will not work.

5. The first person begins and shares their story. It is normal for the mediator to take notes and write the topics that need to be addressed on a central tablet or white board. Each

person gets a turn at sharing their story, uninterrupted, while everyone else listens.

6. The next part of the mediated session is up to the willing-ness of each person to express how they really feel and what they are looking for from the others. Since a lot of pain comes from the belief and experience that others hurt us, it is important that people learn to ask about intentions and understand where they may be coming from. It is equally important to share the impact of the actions that led to the trust violations or conflict. Questions like "What did you mean by..." and "Help me understand..." can help expand understanding of another person's actions.

7. One crucial part of mediation is ensuring that people take the time to understand and acknowledge their impact on other people. Whether it was intentional or not, if another person was hurt because of these actions or inactions, that must be acknowledged, and if an apology is necessary, do that as well. Take the time in this neutral setting to explore these areas and make sure acknowledgment happens.

8. Mediators must let the parties do most of the work. Silence is good, and some struggle to communicate is okay. This mediated session will hopefully set up these people in the future to be able to have conversations together, so they need to develop the skills to talk through issues together. Mediators should intervene if people are going way off track or if any ground rules are being violated. Resist the urge to fix things, and stay away from judgment. Mediators must keep neutrality.

9. As each issue is discussed, identify agreements that people make to resolve the current situation and set them up for success in future interactions. There may be new agreements

on how and when they intend to communicate or some adjustment to behaviors that will enhance the relationships or work processes. The mediator needs to watch that the parties are not giving in too quickly to resolve the situation out of pressure to fix things or fear of facing conflict, otherwise they might agree to something that cannot be sustained.

10. The final step in the mediation process is determining what information, if anything, will be shared outside of the session. Other people will be curious about the mediation, and the stories, feelings, and discussions need to be held in confidence. However, agreements moving forward are usually considered safe to share with others. Again, the mediator will not share anything, but the people involved need to be explicit about what is okay to share outside the sessions.

Ask for a minimum of two hours for the first meeting. Most people want these sessions done in less than an hour, but most of the deeper work comes in the second hour, when they are more comfortable with the process and perhaps more vulnerable. Setting up another session a few days or a week later is also useful because people have time to process their feelings about the new information they may be learning and reflect on their feelings about the issues.

Tool in Action: Mediation

When the vice president of human resources at a medium-sized technology company called me, she was hopeful that I could support two of her managers through some team building consulting and include their entire teams as well. Knowing that disrupted team dynamics is usually a symptom of other things going on, I inquired more specifically about the root cause of the situation with the managers. As she described the events that had led up to the call to me, it was clear that these two managers first needed a neutral space to talk out their concerns without the rest of the team. We agreed to offer mediation to them in a neutral setting with me, and they both agreed. I contacted both in advance with an email and a phone call to describe the process, answer any questions, and do my best to put them both at ease. I also needed to determine that they both were willing participants and that they did not feel forced to enter into the mediation process from the vice president of human resources or anyone else. For mediation to work, they both had to come willingly and be ready to do what they could to move forward.

At the first meeting, Ethan and Melanie shared concerns, examples of times they believed the other person failed them, and what they wanted from each other. While they tried to be professional, there was clearly strain in the relationship and tension in their voices. Their statements were filled with deep emotional hurt that had a strong fixation on the other person causing it. They both appeared to have prepared for this meeting with a long list of offenses the other person had committed with a lot of backup documents.

It turned out that Ethan and Melanie had a rough start at work when they first met. First impressions with some faulty assumptions began the downward spiral of unproductive conversations. When both could not talk straight to each other without interruption or misinterpretation, they moved to the email platform, so conversations could be documented, which only exacerbated the problem when others were copied.

I listened and suspected at the core of the issues were some deeply held beliefs about how people were supposed to act in the workplace, personality style differences, and the need for empathy, especially for the other person to understand what it is like to be in their position. For example, Ethan believed that people needed to earn respect and demonstrate credibility before offering any ideas on improvements. However, Melanie operated at her best when she was generating ideas. She prided herself on being creative; thinking of new ways of doing things was part of her core personality and a reason why she was hired into that position. When Ethan said her ideas barely had merit, she was deeply hurt. You could feel the emotion in the room: hurt, frustration, anger, and resentment.

Ethan believed he considered Melanie's ideas with logic and critical analysis. The more ideas she generated, the more work his group had to do to review and evaluate the plausibility of those ideas. Ethan described his group's workload and his frustration with all the new ideas that started to overwhelm his research team. Ethan also shared a couple of stories of his father, who had drilled into his head that he needed to always hold back his comments until he had credibility with the group. Melanie described her core values of creativity, responsiveness, and openness, and when her ideas were met with walls and pages of reasons why things could not work or not change, she, too, felt frustrated and deflated. With each new piece of information, each new story shared, it shed light on why they treated each other the way they did and why they became so upset.

We reached a point in that first three-hour meeting that they were ready for a break. I suggested they think about what the other person offered and what role they each played in the current situation. I described the need for each person to acknowledge the impacts on others in repairing relationships. But more so, they needed to think about what adjustments they needed to make so that they could help each other bring their best selves to work.

When we met a week later, both seemed more relaxed, and both Ethan and Melanie became more vulnerable through their sharing and discussion. I thought they did some phenomenal work together in this part of the mediation. They began to have some empathy for each other, accepted responsibility, acknowledged their part, and made sincere apologies. The emotional shift in the room was clear, and they became more allies than adversaries. There was still relationship and trust repair work to do, but the shift had been made. They started to generate ideas on how to work together so that they could avoid misunderstandings and decided to meet on a regular basis, just the two of them without everyone else. Ethan agreed to be more open to Melanie's ideas, and Melanie agreed to be conscious of Ethan's workload and work style preferences.

Months after the mediation, both Ethan and Melanie were still adjusting how they worked together, but they had the skills and confidence to work it out together. And in the end, there was no need for the team building as originally requested.

Tool: Video and Discussion: "On Being Wrong"

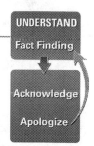

UNDERSTAND
Fact Finding
Acknowledge
Apologize

Purpose

People learn in a number of ways, including realizing that they were wrong about something. Yet, there is a common mindset that admitting mistakes or being wrong is a sign of weakness. When people get stuck in relationships, it is often a matter of holding on to something that they believe is right and others believe is wrong. This polarized view is unhealthy, because there must be room for the possibility that what people believed happened or what others meant by their actions or words can actually be different than their perception.

Kathryn Schulz studies the experience of being wrong. She presented a TED Talk in March 2011 on the subject and reminds her audience that people must be able to entertain the possibility that they could be wrong. Her powerful message prompts rich conversations about the wrong-versus-right phenomenon that if left unexplored keeps people from moving toward more open understanding.

How to Use

- **Individuals:** Watch the video and then read the discussion questions below.

- **Groups:** Show the video and facilitate a discussion about what it means to be right or wrong. Use the questions below as a guide but allow the participants to explore their core beliefs about making mistakes and being wrong.

Steps

1. Watch the TED Talk online by searching for Kathryn Schultz on Being Wrong.[3]

2. Invite discussion about the video:
   - What points stood out to participants?
   - Why is it so hard for people to accept that they could be wrong?

3. Reinforce some key points made by Kathryn Schulz:

   - "Trusting too much in the feeling of being on the correct side of anything can be very dangerous. When we stop entertaining the possibility that we could be wrong, we wind up doing things like...torpedoing the global economy."
   - When people disagree, we tend to think that the other person is:
     - Ignorant: the other person does not have all the facts.
     - Idiot: the other person has the same facts, but they just can't get it put together right.
     - Evil: the person is distorting the data for their own malevolent purposes.
   - This narrow mindset when others disagree with us is a catastrophe. Having the ability to explore issues and disagree means that we are being fully human.

4. Break into groups of two or three people to engage in deeper discussion. Each person has fifteen minutes to explore and respond to the following:

   - Describe a time when you knew you were right and the other person was wrong.

- What are your core beliefs that make you so certain you are right?
- How could your scenario be different if it did not matter who was right or wrong?
- What gets in the way of you staying open to the possibility that you could be wrong?
- What strategies can help you stay open to possibilities rather than polarize who is right or wrong?

5. Debrief as a large group and identify key learning.

6. Discuss as a group and record any agreements on how people can support each other exploring possibilities rather than polarizing who is right and who is wrong.

Source: TED Talk videos online and Kathryn Schulz, "On Being Wrong." Small group discussion questions adapted from Michael Broom and Edith Whitfield Seashore. Used with permission.

Tools to Support the Repair Phase

After you have reached a place where you understand what contributed to the violation of trust, acknowledged your part, and apologized as needed, you may find that you need to engage in some specific activities to repair the root causes of the problems.

Three tools are described in the next several pages that can assist you in the third stage of the Trust Repair Model: Repair. You can use these tools and activities individually or use them with a group.

- Johari Window
- Values Table and Model
- Team Charter

Tool: Johari Window

REPAIR

Engage in Repair Activities

Seek Feedback

Gauge Progress

Create Agreements

Purpose

The Johari Window is a model of awareness in interpersonal relationships that can increase understanding and connectedness between people.

How to Use

- **Individuals:** Read the quadrant descriptions and reflect on yourself. What do you choose to share with others? What do you hold back? How do you receive feedback? What do you think your group needs from you in the "open" area? What are you willing to share to increase what is known by you and others in order to strengthen relationships?

- **Groups:** Describe the purpose of the model and each of the four quadrants. Use examples so others will learn what behaviors, feelings, and motivations go into each of the four quadrants. Break into small groups of 2-4 to discuss the model and its application to the situation. Discuss as a whole group.

This tool works best when it is followed by an interactive activity to invite group members to get to know each other better. There is a small exercise suggestion at the end of the descriptions of the four quadrants of this tool.

Adapted from J. Luft, Group Processes: An Introduction to Group Dynamics, 3rd ed., 1984. Reprinted with permission of McGraw-Hill Education.

Steps

Johari Window

1. Explain the background and purpose of the tool. The Johari Window was created by two American psychologists, Joseph Luft and Harrington Ingham, and it is a model of awareness in interpersonal relations.[4] Knowledge of and using the model can increase awareness, which increases understanding and connectedness between people.

2. Explain the columns and rows: feelings, behaviors, and motivations that are known to self and others and those that are unknown to self and others.

3. **Open area: known to self, known to others.** When things are in the open area we can talk about them. You can walk into someone's workspace and know a little about them if they display photos, mementos of hobbies or interests, sports team memorabilia, or artwork. People may share signage in their yards of the politician they support or wear items that show affiliations to groups like being an alumnus of a university. Making yourself open to others also means sharing some deeper things about yourself—your likes, dislikes, or experiences you have had that have shaped the person you are today. To strengthen connectivity with other people and to build trusting relationships, you need to share some things about yourself with others.

4. **Hidden area: known to self, unknown to others.** Individuals have different personal preferences for what they share with others. People's willingness to disclose and

share information often depends upon the environment and the degree to which others share about themselves. Some people are very private, yet when they share information about themselves, connectivity and empathy increase. Often the level of trust in others is related to what we know about them.

5. **Blind area: unknown to self, known to others.** Others may know something about you that you, yourself are unaware of; therefore, you will need their feedback to eliminate your blind spots. While listening to others' feedback or perceptions about you can make you feel vulnerable, it is an important step to increase awareness and growth. This quadrant can help the entire group strengthen its connectivity by practicing the art of giving and receiving feedback.

6. **Unknown area: unknown to self, unknown to others.** This applies to attitudes and behavior that exist in the person or group, but neither the individual nor the group recognize them. It is what is yet to be discovered. It could be a very creative space to innovate and tap into potential. It can also harbor unresolved problems that an individual or a group is not fully aware of yet. For example, an organization has engineers and auditors who are having great difficulty working together. After investigating the root issues, it turned out that questions of authority and status appeared to be producing bitter feelings from one group to the other. The members of these two groups were unaware of the effects of this problem until they had a shared discovery process and it surfaced.

7. **Dotted lines on the Johari Window.** When people share more about themselves through self-disclosure, the open area enlarges and the hidden area becomes smaller. When feedback is solicited from others, the blind area becomes smaller because you become more aware of your impact

on others. The dotted lines show how the open area can become larger while the other areas adjust accordingly.

Exercise

In pairs, describe a significant experience in your life and explain how the experience affects your values and behavior today. Allow ten minutes per person. After twenty minutes, ask participants to describe the effect that the sharing experience had on their relationship. Do any of them feel more connected? The facilitator helps to relate responses to the Johari quadrants for further learning.

Notes for Further Discussion

- A change in one quadrant will affect each of the others.
- The open area will widen if we have more feedback and disclosure on both sides. A smaller open area will result in poorer communication.
- An increased open area collectively for a whole team means that more of the resources and skills in the group can be applied to the task. You know who can do what.
- There is universal curiosity about the unknown areas of other people, but this is held in check by group norms, training, socialization, and individual abilities.
- Sensitivity means appreciating the covert aspects of behavior and respecting the desire of others to do so.
- When people feel threatened, at risk, or fearful, their open area decreases, their ability to seek feedback for their blind spots decreases, their hidden area grows out of self-protection, and the unknown area, which is their discovery area, is thwarted. Forced awareness is undesirable and usually ineffective.
- Mutual trust increases awareness and can broaden the open area and reduce the size of the other areas.

Tool in Action: Johari Window

Johari Window

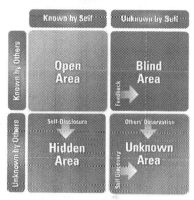

The Johari Window is a valuable concept. I use it as a prelude to getting-to-know-you activities whenever I find people who need to strengthen their relationships. The use of the tool became critical when an executive team hired me to support their trust repair efforts and improve their ability to work together. After interviewing each executive leader, it was clear to me that despite working together for many years, they barely knew each other. And I knew that without strong connectivity, this group would be less efficient and subject to problems no matter how hard they tried.

We organized a two-day off-site meeting where I dedicated the majority of the time to building their connectivity. I shared the Johari Window and examples for each quadrant. I also reviewed articles I gave them to read in advance of the meeting. These articles included research supporting strengthening team efficacy when people knew each other on a more personal level. The executives' discussion surrounding these articles were mixed, with some seeing the value of sharing more about themselves and others believing that what is personal should stay private. I then moved into an activity designed to invite each person to tell their life story through a series of structured questions that they could answer at length in whatever capacity they wanted. To demonstrate the level of vulnerability desired, I began and modeled by telling my story and the events in my life that have shaped the person I am today. Then, each person had a chance to share their story in an uninterrupted manner.

The tension in the air was noticeably different from the first moment we started until the last person ended. I asked, "What was common or different or what struck you in the stories you heard?" "How did listening to others inform how you perceived them?" Their comments were astonishing. "I never knew you experienced that as a woman of color." "I see that we are both military brats; moving around a lot made it hard to make friends." "I never really thought about how certain experiences in my life have influenced my leadership and communication style."

I asked the group to consider how their Johari Windows shifted after this experience and conversation. Several expressed that the open area expanded and that they believed that it would help them work better together now that they had more information, context, empathy, and things in common with each other. I also asked about what went into their decision about what to share and what they chose to keep to themselves in their hidden area. The group discussed safety and strong belief systems regarding what personal information is shared or not shared at work. They continued the discussion about what they could do to keep connectivity strong and support expanding their open areas by generating and agreeing to some new group norms.

The next set of questions regarded how they individually sought feedback and how they experienced it as a team. After having such a strong morning opening up and getting to know each other, the group was able to discuss their current methods surrounding feedback, and their verdict was they needed a lot of work. There was aversion to giving direct feedback to each other for fear of retribution and fear of losing relationships. Those who previously provided feedback did not provide it in the best manner.

I shared principles of feedback and helped the group practice it with each other. There were some vulnerable moments, but at the end of the day, because they had created a space together to discuss experiences, they made significant progress toward giving and receiving feedback.

To solidify the learning and open the door to new possibilities, the group discussed the value of the unknown area, which is a discovery area, and what they needed to do to create the space where they could learn together. The executive team made new commitments, generated new working agreements, put into place new formal and informal feedback mechanisms for themselves, and met their goal of strengthening relationships and improving trust.

One executive summarized at the end, "I didn't think it was possible to improve our situation. Honestly, I was secretly annoyed that we would be spending so much time here today doing touchy-feely stuff. I came in a skeptic, but I am leaving feeling more optimistic. I never really thought that the core issue between us was that we didn't really know much about each other and therefore that affected how we were willing to work together and help each other out. I know each of us have to make this happen, so we are not out of the woods yet. I want to have a better functioning team. Our employees, shareholders, and customers need us to function exceptionally well. We owe this to them and to each other."

Tool: Values Table

Purpose

People have a tendency to operate out of a core set of values that drive their behaviors. Often people are operating from a good place, but sometimes their behaviors adversely affect others. People are more likely to hold on to their current behaviors if they believe they are being principled. The Values Table bridges understanding between core values, the behaviors people use to act on those values, and the results others experience from the behaviors.

When you experience behaviors, actions, and inactions and have results that are worrisome, explore the values at play. Holding conversations about the results of the behaviors becomes easier when you discover the values underlying them. And when people understand the core values at play, they are more empathetic and will want to see other people succeed. The true leverage is to focus on adjusting behaviors and help people see the impact of their actions. People have the ability to adjust their behaviors to get different results while still holding on to their core values.

How to Use

- **Individuals:** Read the column descriptions below and think about some behaviors that are getting results that you do not like. Write them in the appropriate columns. Think about possible core values that may be contributing to the situation. Can you then think of other possible behaviors that will yield different results? Consider having discussions with others about your reflections.

- **Groups:** On a large board or sheet of paper, draw out the Values Table and label the three columns. Give one or two examples (see below) with the group to demonstrate the tool. Always start with the middle column—the behaviors—then solicit ideas about the possible results of those behaviors. Ask the group to think about possible core values underlying the behaviors. Then invite examples of behaviors that the group finds troublesome and record the impacts from those behaviors. Ask what core values are driving these behaviors, and use the group members to verify or adjust the words. Get the group to generate new behaviors that will yield different results all while honoring the core values indicated. Keep the conversation going until every person gets clarity about the most pressing issues facing them.

Steps

1. Begin with the middle column by listing behaviors, actions, or inactions that people are experiencing. Be as specific as possible.

2. In the results column, list the results of those behaviors. What's happening because of them? This is a great place to get multiple perspectives because people can experience different results from the behaviors exhibited in column 2.

3. List the likely core values underlying the behaviors—think positively here. This is a powerful reframe and will help you hold conversations about adjusting behaviors to yield different results, all while honoring core values.

4. Use the word *adjust* rather than *change*. People are more willing to adjust behaviors rather than change who they are and what they believe. The word *change* tells our brains something different than the word *adjust*. Adjusting is more palatable, and people feel they remain in control.

Values	Behaviors/Actions	Results
Honesty	"Brutally honest" "Tell it like it is" without any filter	✓ Hurt feelings ✓ Shock ✓ Don't want to work with that person anymore

The core value of honesty is a value most people can buy into. However, when people are brutally honest or say things without any filter, feelings can get hurt, and there are repercussions in the group.

This exercise is not about asking the person to change their core value; rather, the leverage comes when they can see the impact of how they act out their value and its impact on others. In order to get different results, the change comes from adjusting behaviors, not values. This happens with feedback from others about the results of those behaviors and staying in the conversation about other possible behaviors that will get different results that everyone can buy into.

We can only make assumptions regarding the core values of others. The key is having a conversation and talking about it. Use this tool to help guide that conversation.

Values	Behaviors/Actions	Results
Honesty	"Let me offer some advice based on my experience of what inspectors look for…" "Please make this section stronger in your written report because…"	✓ Learning ✓ Things typically change based on the honest review or feedback ✓ Strengthens relationships

Tool in Action: Values Table

The stories were hard to hear through the tears and frustrated words of team members. A manager asked me to work with this team to find out why they were falling apart. After interviewing each person, it was clear the team members were unhappy with the supervisor and explicitly pointed out several behaviors that were undermining productivity and morale. However, when I interviewed the supervisor, he was adamant that his actions were grounded in integrity and upholding high work standards.

Using the Values Table, I drew the three columns on an easel pad and placed in the first column words like "strong work ethic" and "happiness." I did this intentionally to highlight what I believed to be core values of both the supervisor and of many of the team members. In the center column, I wrote out the behaviors that people described during the interviews.

Values	Behaviors/Actions	Results
Strong work ethic	Supervisor left Post-it notes on workers' desks at 8:00, 12:00, 1:00, and 5:00 if they were not present. Expected leave slips to be turned in for every six minutes not at workplace (one-tenth of an hour in the leave system).	
Happiness	Social time in morning and end of day to greet and connect with co-workers. Potlucks, parties for birthdays, recognition events.	

Next, I asked each person to write out what they are experiencing as the results from these behaviors. There were no right or wrong responses here. It is an important part of acknowledging the impact of other's actions and behaviors without judgment.

Supervisor's Perceived Results from the Behaviors

Values	Behaviors/Actions	Results
Strong work ethic	Supervisor left Post-it notes on workers' desks at 8:00, 12:00, 1:00, and 5:00 if they were not present. Expected leave slips to be turned in for every six minutes not at workplace (one-tenth of an hour in the leave system).	✓ Compliance improved showing people adhere to work hours (Supervisor) ✓ All hours are worked or accounted for; therefore, we are honoring our job commitments
Happiness	Social time in morning and end of day to greet and connect with co-workers. Potlucks, parties for birthdays, recognition events.	✓ Increased annoyance when they take too much time talking because it reduces productivity

Employee/Worker Perceived Results from the Behaviors

Values	Behaviors/Actions	Results
Strong work ethic	Supervisor left Post-it notes on workers' desks at 8:00, 12:00, 1:00, and 5:00 if they were not present. Expected leave slips to be turned in for every six minutes not at workplace (one-tenth of an hour in the leave system).	✓ Anger ✓ Loss of respect ✓ Frustration ✓ Feel minimized ✓ Lack of understanding ✓ Micromanaged
Happiness	Social time in morning and end of day to greet and connect with co-workers. Potlucks, parties for birthdays, recognition events.	✓ Huge source of joy ✓ Better connections between people ✓ Getting to know others breaks down barriers to communication and prevents misunderstanding, resulting in increased productivity

When both the supervisor and employees shared their lists, they were surprised. How could their experiences be so different? People commented on the lists and found that the link to an underlying core value was both plausible and interesting. An important step here is to have people listen to each other and see the full linkage between a person's core value—how they enact that value through behaviors—and then the result.

If they didn't like the results but could buy into the core value (which most people can at the core value level), the leverage for change is to adjust the behaviors.

Employees opened up about how leaving Post-it notes on their desks was demoralizing. Several offered many stories and explanations and wanted the supervisor to understand that even though they were not physically present at their workstation, it did not mean that they were not working. The supervisor did not mean to cause harm and said so. He engaged with the team about other ways he could demonstrate and uphold his core value of a strong work ethic. The group came up with new agreements, including the discussion around potlucks and other social activities, and left the meeting satisfied that they each had been heard.

As with most groups after living with the new agreements for a while, adjustments were needed as they evolved as a group and new situations emerged. This group did a good job of checking in with each other and respecting that people were starting from a values-centered place and that the rest (behaviors and actions) was negotiable. They integrated new people into their team and shared the Values Table with them, so they could also engage in conversation from a place of understanding. This group used this method for several years and kept it in the forefront because they had experienced such a negative period of time and did not want to relive it.

The gift of this tool is that you are not asking someone to change their core values. Rather, through understanding the impact your actions have on others, you can each make necessary adjustments to get a better outcome while staying true to what matters most to you.

Tool: Team Charter

Purpose

A charter is a written agreement that spells out the purpose and expectations given to a team and the responsibilities of all the people involved.

How to Use

- **Individuals:** While charter documents are typically used as agreements between a group and its sponsor, individuals can review the question prompts as a guide to organizing their own projects or to be better-prepared team members when their group is going through the chartering process.

- **Groups:** Creating a charter is a must for group projects and assignments. A charter should be discussed, agreed to, and then signed by all the members of the team, the management sponsors, and other appropriate people before the team starts working.

The charter should include the following elements at a minimum:

- A description of the issue that the team is to address or the reason for their existence.
- All expected outcomes of the team effort.
- All parameters relevant to the effort: staff resources available, use of a facilitator, available or required training, technical support available, deadlines or time constraints, other groups that need to be consulted, options that are off the table, and decision-making authorities.
- Decision-making process to be used by the team.

- Method by which the team will communicate with management and other key stakeholders.
- Names, roles, and responsibilities of all team members, management sponsors, the facilitator, and other appropriate people.

The team agreements worksheet that follows the charter is for the team to use. Teams should cover some of the elements in the agreements, such as encouraged group behaviors and norms, meeting frequency, conflict strategies, and roles of individual members. While not all of the sections are relevant to each team, working through them will help the team address problems in advance. It is up to the individual team to decide which sections they wish to use.

Steps

1. Give an overview of the work this team will do: purpose, scope of work, expected outcomes (e.g., no complaints from customers), key processes and functions for which they are responsible, boundaries, constraints, and limitations.

2. Explain why the team's work is important to this organization and why each team member was selected.

3. Share background information that may be relevant. For example, what is going on in the organization that may be important to the team's work plan? Provide customer information, requirements, and needs that may help the team's efforts.

4. The draft language of the charter can begin with the management sponsor. Once the sponsor has completed the draft, it is sent to the team for review and input. If there are any changes or questions, the sponsor and the team work it

out until there is a clear understanding on both sides. Once the language is satisfactory to everyone, then they all sign it.

Pitfalls

Without a charter, the team risks going off in a direction that does not have the support of management. Without spelling out the roles and responsibilities, things can fall through the cracks or be duplicated. The team agreements set out the group norms, without which the team misses a critical step in the formation of any team. Working through the norms prompts discussion about accountability, communication paths, schedules, and other logistical and interpersonal items that are necessary for the team to function efficiently.

Team Charter Worksheet

This is an agreement between _____ (sponsor) and the members of the _____ team.

The members of the team are:

_____ (sponsor) has given our team the following charge:

Our purpose is important to the success of the program mission or goals because:

To succeed in our charge, we are responsible for developing, conducting and continuously improving the following key processes:

For each of those processes, _____ (sponsor) expects certain measurable results. The following is a list of the results to be obtained for each process and the way that we will measure our progress toward achieving those results:

_____ (sponsor) will help ensure our success by working with us to obtain the resources we need to carry out our purpose. At this time, the resources needed are:

_____ (sponsor) has authorized us to make the following decisions as a team:

_____ (sponsor) has asked that we consult with them before making the following decisions:

We will communicate with _____ (sponsor) by:

We will communicate with other key stakeholders (managers, board members, partners) by:

List any other agreements made between the team and the sponsor:

In signing this charter, we are committing ourselves to work as a team in concert with our sponsor to accomplish our purpose and support the vision, mission, values and goals of this organization.

(Signatures of team members and sponsor)

Source: Mary Campbell[5] and Wendy Fraser.

Team Agreements Worksheet

PURPOSE
The name of our team is:

Our mission, according to the charter with our sponsor, is to:

TEAM LEADER
Who is the team leader?

What do we expect of the team leader?

TEAM MEMBER BEHAVIOR
How will we treat and interact with each other? What behaviors are encouraged? What behaviors are taboo?

How will we interact and communicate with our internal customers?

What principles will guide our interactions with our external customers? How will we communicate with them?

What principles will guide our interactions with our stakeholders? How will we communicate with them?

MEETINGS, TEAM FACILITATOR, TEAM RECORDER

When, where and how often will we meet as a team?

How will we develop the meeting agenda?

What ground rules will we use during the meeting?

Who will facilitate meetings?

Who will record the decisions/assignments/things to follow up on?

Is there a timeline for sharing the recorded meeting notes?

Who receives the meeting notes?

What will we do if we think we need a special team meeting?

FOLLOW-THROUGH

What can we expect from each other when we have assignments?

When push comes to shove on priorities, how will we handle conflicts?

OTHER ROLES

What other roles are assigned to team members? (List each role, the person to whom assigned, and the expectations the team has of that person.)

MAKING DECISIONS

What kinds of decisions can be made by an individual team member?

What kinds of decisions must be brought to the whole team?

How will we make decisions as a team?

How do we define *consensus*?

What will we do if we cannot reach a consensus? How will we support team decisions even if we don't 100 percent agree with them?

CONFLICT

How will we address conflict between team members?

When should we seek help with a conflict? From whom?

EVALUATING OUR WORK
When and how often will we evaluate our work?

What process will we use to evaluate our work?

CLOSURE
How will we celebrate our work?

What process will we use to bring closure to our team?

Source: Mary Campbell and Wendy Fraser.

Tool in Action: Team Charter

I cannot stress enough the importance of a team charter. Whenever I have been talked out of using one, it has always come back to bite me. Sometimes groups think they are clear about their purpose and work, or sometimes they think they all just know how to get along and do not need to write anything down to specify expected behaviors. They inevitably hit a storming stage where members argue about the true purpose of their work or there are behaviors that are disrupting the group, but because they did not take the time to spell out which behaviors helped or hindered them, they waste time and energy on fixing it later. There is a propensity to skip these steps and just get into the "real business" of the meeting. But facilitators, leaders, and team members must persevere and take time to clarify the parameters of the work before moving forward.

I use team charters with small assignments with just a few people. I modify the charter to include only the relevant parts to the assignment. Clearly understanding the purpose, roles, expectations, communication preferences, deadlines, and decision-making authority is paramount in any assignment or project.

When my daughter left for college, I suggested that she use some of the team agreements questions with her roommate, paying particular attention to the parts about how they intended to interact with each other (e.g., good behaviors, taboo behaviors). They discussed, in advance, the ways they would work out disagreements and conflicts. Having a plan early will help them later when they experience some difficult moments, which inevitably happen whenever you live with someone.

When groups struggle, always return to the basics and review the charter. If there is no charter, create one, even if the team is already engaged in the project cycle. If a team is struggling, this could be an indicator that something changed and requires charter modifications. Consider:

- Has the scope changed?
- Have expectations been adjusted?
- Have communication needs and decision-making agreements changed?
- Has personnel changed? Members leaving/new members joining?

Any one of these indicators signals a need to review and update the charter.

Tools to Support the Evolve Phase

After you have engaged in specific activities designed to repair the source problems, you will need to let things evolve into a new normal.

The following pages describe tools to assist in the fourth state of the Trust Repair Model: Evolve. These tools are designed for individual and/or group use:

- Check-Ins and Check-Outs
- Evaluation

Tool: Check-Ins and Check-Outs

Purpose

Understanding where people are at as they enter and leave groups is an essential piece of information for effective group functioning. Check-ins are a deliberate communication and relationship-strengthening technique that are done at the beginning of meetings or gatherings that help people transition their minds, hearts, and energy from where they have been into the present as they join the group. For example, if someone has a rough morning, it helps other group members know that the behaviors that person is demonstrating have to do with something outside of the group rather than inside the group. This information can often avert hurt feelings and misperception.

Check-ins build community and strengthen relationships as people get a chance to get their voice in the room, and each time they do it, they share a little bit more about themselves with others. This process builds connection and informs others about their concerns, ideas, and any preoccupations they may bring with them to a session. It is a great way for facilitators and leaders to gauge the group's energy and opinion about subjects, because check-in questions can be tailored to match the group session.

Check-outs are a technique done at the end of a meeting or gathering that allows each person to express thoughts as the session ends. Simple check-outs include using one word to describe how they are feeling or what they are thinking as they leave. They could check out by sharing one new idea that resonated with them that day or one question they are still grappling with in their minds. Check-outs help leaders and facilitators gauge the session's impact on people and the content.

How to Use

- **Individuals:** Check-ins and check-outs are usually for groups of two or more people. However, individuals can reflect at the start of their day with a check-in and explore their feelings and thoughts about relationships and work assignments, and similarly at the end the of the day with reflective self-check-outs.

- **Groups:** Use check-ins and check-outs each time a group gets together, no matter the size of the group. If facilitating a large group (more than thirty), request check-ins via smaller subgroups or table groups. With smaller groups, tailor check-in and check-out questions to provide feedback about the group's work progress or invite people to freely express what they want to as they start the meeting. Do not skip check-ins or check-outs to save time. When people feel more connected to the group and to each other, the work of the group gets easier, and this will save time in the long run.

Steps

1. Invite each person to express any thoughts as the group comes together. The meeting organizer asks specific questions prompts to allow each person to determine what to share during the check-in. For example:
   - "Say your name, organization, and what you would like to get out of the training session today."
   - "What most excites and concerns you about [subject of the meeting]."
   - "How did you use the tools/information that we covered last month?"
   - "How are you doing as you come into the group today?"

2. Remind people that check-ins and check-outs are not a discussion. Ensure that no one can interrupt the speaker or respond until everyone has finished their turn. Instruct group members that if they feel like interrupting or making a comment, they should hold their comments until everyone has finished. This way, they stay present with what the person is saying and do not get preoccupied with what they want to ask, comment on, or further discuss.

3. Describe the check-ins and check-outs process choices. They can go quickly in a circle fashion around the room, around individual tables, randomly as each person wishes to speak, or with the last speaker calling on the next person to speak.

4. Solicit additional comments and input once everyone has completed the check-in process. If there are none, start the meeting agenda.

Adapted from Charles Seashore and Edith Whitfield Seashore.[6] Used with permission.

Tool in Action: Check-Ins and Check-Outs

I co-facilitate an in-depth (and amazingly impactful) leadership development program in which participants meet for two days every month. We use the check-in and check-out tool each day to strengthen relationships and to help us gather information from everyone about how they are doing as they enter the learning environment. To bridge theory with practice, we ask participants to use the tools in between our monthly learning sessions and report back on their experiences.

One leader described how she chose to use a check-in with youth soccer players before a game in a moment when other coaches were running drills, and it made a huge impact. This leader is an exceptional, well-credentialed soccer coach, with great intellect and charisma. It is clear she knows the soccer business and how to prepare players for the game. At the last minute, she was designated to travel with a club team with fill-in players coming from all over the state. Many of the players did not know each other; this coach realized she needed to assist these girls to work effectively as a team. Due to unforeseen circumstances, they arrived at the field of their first game twenty minutes before start time. Instead of running drills for twenty minutes, this coach chose to have the girls sit down and do a check-in and get to know each other for fifteen minutes. "I knew that they would hesitate passing the ball to other players they didn't know. Players have to have a sense about other players. I had them check in with their names, schools, and some fun facts about themselves. Then, we talked about how we wanted to play together and sort of generated a vision for the game."

Even with less than five minutes to warm up and run a few drills, the girls started the game with stronger connections than when they arrived on the field. They played like they had known each other for a long time, even though they had never met before that day. "It was phenomenal. We won the game. But more so, it solidified in me the need to do check-ins and check-outs even when you feel you don't have time to spare. I knew then that this is what has been missing with my teams. Now, I start every practice and game with a check-in!"

I also teach a 120-hour Lean Six Sigma Black Belt course. We meet twelve full days over a few months, and every day I use the check-in and check-out tool. I have experienced, on multiple occasions, student personnel from organizations in manufacturing, military, government, and corporate entities who wonder why I take a lot of time to conduct a long check-in in our first class. I choose to use more in-depth questions whenever a group is meeting for the first time so they can get to know each other. I take a couple of hours to let people introduce themselves and orient themselves to the group and topic of learning. While there is some uneasiness about the amount of time dedicated to getting to know each other, people feel that at the end of these check-ins that the group has changed. People are more comfortable with each other; they are less anxious and feel more connected. After that, we have normal check-ins and check-outs for our meeting days.

I am always delighted to hear from some Black Belt students about how they use this tool in their organizations and personal lives. One man shared that he implemented it on the manufacturing floor with his team and believes it has increased their productivity because people are more willing to speak up about issues and feel safe when suggesting changes. Another man found that he got better results with his CrossFit class whenever he had the exercise participants check in. They felt less embarrassed and more supported and tried harder in the exercises.

At the end of sessions, I particularly enjoy listening to the check-out comments from participants. This gives me sound information about what they gleaned, what they found most or least important, or what topics may still be on their minds. Check-out comments help me plan better for the next session and identify issues that need follow-up.

These are just a few of many success stories confirming the positive impacts from using the check-in and check-out tools. They are easy to use, can be initiated at any time and clearly bolster your work to build trust and strengthen relationships.

Tool: Evaluation

EVOLVE

Move Forward

Forgive

Learn, Grow and Evolve

Honor Agreements

Appreciate

Purpose

An evaluation is a deeper and intentional check on how the relationships have progressed since trust repair efforts went into action. It is important to understand the impact of the changes and agreements to date and make adjustments if needed. Evaluations and the conversations that go along with them allow for the relationships to continue to evolve.

How to Use

- **Individuals:** Reflect on the questions personally and make notes. While this tool is geared toward conversations between people who have had trust issues and have been trying to work it out, individuals can benefit by reflecting on the questions at any time.

- **Groups:** Share the questions in advance and invite each person to first reflect on their own. It is best to give at least a day or more for people to reflect adequately and to be ready for the conversation. Discuss the questions and listen to each person's point of view. Celebrate and appreciate the progress. Acknowledge each person's experience. Discuss and make adjustments in how you work together moving forward. You may need to update team charter language or other agreements. Remind everyone that it is natural for groups to evolve and your working agreements may need updating to reflect changes.

Steps

1. Assess and discuss how the relationships have changed. Consider the state your relationships were in:

    a. Before the trust violation happened

    b. When the trust violations were occurring

    c. During the trust repair activities

    d. After the trust repair activities to the present

2. How are you the same? How are you different?

3. How is your group the same? How is your group different?

4. Have the relationships deepened? If so, how? If not, why?

5. In what way was it worth trying to repair? What difference did it make?

6. How are things working right now? What is going well and what adjustments need to be made to move forward?

7. What have you learned about yourself? Whether or not all the agreements have been kept, you have come out in a different place.

Stay hopeful. Every relationship has challenges and all relationships have potential to evolve into something better. Perhaps ten years from now, you will laugh about a current situation that perplexes you. Allow yourself and others to grow, make mistakes, recover, and make amends. Make the choice and be intentional about strengthening relationships with others. When you do, the world will be a brighter place and you will be healthier and happier. Remember, trust repair *is* possible!

ACKNOWLEDGMENTS

As I complete this book and reflect on the journey, I am indebted to my Creator for the ability to write and teach others how to strengthen trust. My hope is that this work will make a positive difference in fostering healthy human relationships. I am humbled and grateful to all the mentors, teachers, and family members who have come before me and have laid a path so that I may succeed. I believe my work builds on their wisdom, and I graciously pass it forward to others so that it may be of service in their relationships. I am grateful for the friendship and mentorship of the late Edie Seashore, from whom I drew deep inspiration and learned how to pay attention to human interaction in groups. Her work lives on through me, and I am a better human being for knowing her and working with her.

I am enormously grateful to my original trust study participants, who entrusted me with their stories. Their willingness to share their experiences about trust laid the groundwork for my research and inspired me to stay curious and open to learning about how to help people repair damaged trust. I also am grateful to the thousand-plus people who provided input on the trust behaviors in workshops and discussions. My Fielding Graduate University professors and doctoral committee members guided and sharpened my research with their tenacious questions and focus on quality. Thank you to Dr. Barbara Mink, Dr. Frank Barrett, Dr. Roy Lewicki, Dr. Shawn O'Fallon, and the late Dr. Charles Seashore.

There were several key people who provided support, wisdom,

encouragement, challenge, humor, and glasses of red wine. Thank you to Karen Schoessel, who provided most of first draft editing and had an eagle eye for grammar and sentence structure. My deep appreciation also goes out to Mary Beth Colón, Louise Doran, Tina Fortuna, Will Rice, and Matthew Savolskis, who also read and edited drafts. And to the first group of friends and colleagues whom I asked to read the initial chapters to make sure it made sense; your early feedback was extremely helpful: Mary Campbell, Dian Christian, Tess Fox, Linda Hall, Rosalund Jenkins, Sandra Kinoshita, Sammie Mack, Lynn Neeley, and Debbie Rough-Mack. My dear friends Fr. Kilian Malvey, Kristin Skarie, Maureen Huentelman, Danae Barrett, Jacki Burgener, Don Conant, Shelley Dahle, Bill Dahle, Daya Fields, Rosalund Jenkins, and Lori Schumacher graciously listened to me and provided support as I contemplated writing this book. And I appreciate my Triple Impact colleagues Dr. Gwen Kennedy, Dr. Michael Broom, Evan Hall, Anita Bhasin, and all the participants over the years for being a collective support system for this trust repair work.

My book club, Away With Words, read an early draft of the book and provided a great evening of conversation and candid feedback. While this group of women are inspiring, intelligent, and wickedly fun, they challenged my thinking and helped me to improve my writing and the book. Thank you to all the members, but especially Julie Forth, Mary Janelle Cady, Heidi Cope, Molly Drescher, Linda Hall, Amy Hatch-Winecka, Iryna Nath, Karen Ordos, Jennifer Vachon, Maribel Vilchez, and Ann Willis for reading the book draft and joining the evening's conversation.

I had a wonderful support in the creation of this book. Connie Lovelady, Graphic Concepts, Inc., sat with me multiple times at a coffee shop as I described the models and images I wanted to convey. I appreciate her creativity, patience, and professionalism. Apryle Donato captured video and provided my first video for the book and website. And photographer Doug Walker set up on a hot spring afternoon and took some amazing pictures of my work. And a huge shout out to Jenni Robbins with Ignite Development, Inc., for her outstanding support and wisdom in shaping my business strategy and expert positioning for this trust repair work in the world. I am thankful to the SiteCrafting website development team for their professionalism and creativity in building a site that reflects this important work in the world. Finally, I appreciate Lori Paximadis's keen eyes and copyediting abilities to polish this manuscript and make it ready for publication.

I asked a group of colleagues and friends to support the creation of the video, and they enthusiastically agreed. My heartfelt appreciation goes to: Tammy Anderson, Tim Anderson, Darien Babauta, Cyndee Baugh, Amy Besel, Lauren Burnes, Mary Campbell, Patrick Carnahan, Elizabeth Colón, Mary Beth Colón, Rafael Colón, Heidi Cope, Rogelio Cortes, Shelley Dahle, Megan Davis, Louise Doran, Julie Forth, Tess Fox, Alyson Fouts, John Fraser, Noemi LaChapelle, Edmon Lee, Nicole Morales, Lynn Neeley, Jon Noski, Christopher Reading, Debbie Rough-Mack, Matthew Savolskis, Karen Schoessel, Dr. Solomon Uwadalie, Chastity Walck, Dr. Matondo Wawa, and Sam Wilson.

Finally, I am so lucky to have such a loving, supportive, and fun family. My life partner and husband John, son Tristan, and daughter Maren...you are all my rock and keepers of my heart. A shout out to my sisters, Stacey, Jodie, and Tiffany, and my brothers, Steve and Jason, thanks for your texts and support. I love you all very much!

I have not attempted to cite in the text all the authorities and sources consulted in the preparation of this book. To do so would require more space than is available. The list would include departments of various organizations, libraries, and many individuals. To write it, I relied upon my doctoral research, applied practice and consulting with clients over the years, and twenty-five years of working with groups to help them be as effective as possible. I have changed names and organization identifiers to keep anonymity.

REFERENCES

Introduction

1. C. Bergland, "Holding a Grudge Produces Cortisol and Diminishes Oxytocin," *Psychology Today*, April 11, 2015.
2. Gallup, *State of the American Workplace*, 2017.
3. M. Beck, "The Key to Healing Emotional Wounds," *Oprah Magazine*, November 2016.

Chapter 1

1. J. B. Rotter, "Generalized Expectancies for Interpersonal Trust," *American Psychologist* 26, no. 5 (1971): 443–452, at 443.
2. S. McLeod, "Erik Erikson's Stages of Psychosocial Development," SimplyPsychology.org, May 3, 2018, https://www.simplypsychology.org/Erik-Erikson.html.
3. D. H. McKnight, L. L. Cummings, and H. L. Chervany, "Initial Trust Formation and New Organizational Relationships," *Academy of Management Review* 23, no. 3 (1998): 473–490; R. M. Kramer and R. J. Lewicki, "Repairing and Enhancing Trust: Approaches to Reducing Organizational Trust Deficits," *Academy of Management Annals* 4, no. 1 (2010): 245–277.

4. W. H. Jones and M. P. Burdette, "Betrayal in Relationships," in *Perspectives on Close Relationships*, ed. A. L. Weber and J. H. Harvey (Boston: Allyn and Bacon, 1994).

5. A. R. Elangovan and D. L. Shapiro, "Betrayal of Trust in Organizations," *Academy of Management Review* 23, no. 3 (1998): 547–566.

6. C. Duhigg, "What Google Learned from Its Quest to Build the Perfect Team," *New York Times* online, February 25, 2016.

7. A. C. Edmondson, "Psychological Safety, Trust, and Learning in Organizations: A Group-Level Lens," in *Trust and Distrust in Organizations: Dilemmas and Approaches*, vol. 7, ed. R. M. Kramer and K. S. Cook (New York: Sage, 2004), p. 241.

8. R. M. Kramer, "Divergent Realities and Convergent Disappointments in the Hierarchic Relation: Trust and the Intuitive," in *Trust in Organizations: Frontiers in Theory and Research*, ed. R. M. Kramer and T. R. Tyler (Thousand Oaks, CA: Sage, 1996).

9. R. C. Mayer, M. B. Davis, and F. D. Schoorman, "An Integrative Model of Organizational Trust," *Academy of Management Review* 20, no. 3 (1995): 709–734; K. T. Dirks and D. L. Ferrin, "Trust in Leadership: Meta-Analytic Findings and Implications for Research and Practice," *Journal of Applied Psychology* 87, no. 4 (2002): 611–628.

10. K. T. Dirks and D. P. Skarlicki, "Trust in Leaders: Existing Research and Emerging Issues," in *Trust and Distrust in Organizations: Dilemmas and Approaches*, vol. 7, ed. R. M. Kramer and K. S. Cook (New York: Sage, 2004).

Chapter 2

1. W. L. Fraser, "Trust Violation and Repair: An Exploration of the Views of Work Group Members," PhD thesis, Fielding Graduate University, 2010.

2. W. Oncken, Jr. and D. L. Wass, "Management Time: Who's Got the Monkey?" Harvard Business Review, November-December, 1999.

Chapter 4

1. V. Anderson and L. Johnson, *Systems Thinking Basics: From Concepts to Causal Loops* (Waltham, MA: Pegasus Communications, 1997).
2. R. Boyatzis and D. Goleman, *Emotional and Social Competency Inventory* (Philadelphia: Hay Group, 2007).
3. K. Lewin, *Principles of Topological Psychology* (New York: McGraw-Hill, 1936).
4. T. Menon and L. Thompson, "Putting a Price on People Problems at Work. *Harvard Business Review*, August 23, 2016.
5. B. Zeigarnik, "Das Behalten erledigter und unerledigter Handlungen," *Psychologische Forschung* 9 (1927): 1–85.

Chapter 5

1. R. Vitelli, "Remembering 9/11: How Accurate Are "Flashbulb Memories" of Tragic Events in our Recent History?" *Psychology Today* online, March 23, 2015.
2. R. J. Lewicki, B. Polin, and R. B. Lount Jr., "An Exploration of the Structure of Effective Apologies," *Negotiation and Conflict Management Research* 9, no. 2 (2016): 177–196.
3. C. W. Moore, *The Mediation Process: Practical Strategies for Resolving Conflict*, 4th ed. (San Francisco: Jossey-Bass, 2014).
4. R. J. Lewicki and E. C. Tomlinson, "Trust, Trust Development, and Trust Repair," in *The Handbook of Conflict Resolution. Theory and Practice*, 3rd ed., ed. P. T. Coleman, M. Deutsch, and E. C. Marcus (San Francisco: Jossey-Bass, 2014).

Chapter 6

1. D. Bargal, "Personal and Intellectual Influences Leading to Lewin's Paradigm of Action Research: Towards the 60th Anniversary of Lewin's 'Action Research and Minority Problems' (1946)," *Action Research* 4 (2006): 367.
2. C. Duhigg, "What Google Learned from Its Quest to Build the Perfect Team," *New York Times* online, February 25, 2016.
3. C. N. Seashore, E. W. Seashore, and G. M. Weinberg, *What Did You Say? The Art of Giving and Receiving Feedback*, 10th ed. (Columbia: Bingham House Books, 2003).
4. H. Ren and B. Gray, "Repairing Relationship Conflict: How Violation Types and Culture Influence the Effectiveness of Restoration Rituals," *Academy of Management Review* 34, no. 1 (2009): 105–126.

Chapter 7

1. M. M. Tugade and B. L. Fredrickson, "Resilient Individuals Use Positive Emotions to Bounce Back from Negative Emotional Experiences," *Journal of Personality and Social Psychology* 86 (2004): 320–333.
2. C. N. Seashore, *Developing and Using Personal Support Systems*, National Training Lab (NTL) Reading Book for Human Relations Training, 1982.
3. R. D. Enright, *8 Keys to Forgiveness* (New York: W. W. Norton and Company, 2015), p. 13
4. R. D. Enright, *8 Keys to Forgiveness* (New York: W. W. Norton and Company, 2015), p. 31
5. J. J. Exline and R. F. Baumeister, "Expressing Forgiveness and Repentance: Benefits and Barriers," in *Forgiveness: Theory, Research, and Practice*, ed. M. E. McCullough, K. I. Pargament, and C. E. Thoresen (New York: Gilford Press, 2000); H. M.

Wallace, J. J. Exline, and R. F. Baumeister, "Interpersonal Consequences of Forgiveness: Does Forgiveness Deter or Encourage Repeat Offenses?" *Journal of Experimental Social Psychology* 44 (2008): 453–460.

Chapter 8

1. W. L. Fraser, "Trust Violation and Repair: An Exploration of the Views of Work Group Members," PhD thesis, Fielding Graduate University, 2010.

Chapter 9

1. L. Davey, L. "Managing Two People Who Hate Each Other," *Harvard Business Review* online, June 9, 2014.
2. Ibid.

Chapter 10

1. E. W. Seashore, *The Choice Matrix*, 2006, permission granted from the Seashore family.
2. C. Argryis, *Overcoming Organizational Defenses: Facilitating Organizational Learning*, 1ˢᵗ ed. (Upper Saddle River, NJ: Pearson Education, 1990), used with permission; material also includes concepts from P. M. Senge, A. Kleiner, C. Roberts, R. B. Ross, and B. J. Smith, "Ladder of Inference," in *The Fifth Discipline Fieldbook: Strategies and Tools for Building a Learning Organization* (New York: Doubleday, 1994), used with permission.
3. K. Schulz, "On Being Wrong," TED Talks online, March 2011, https://www.ted.com/talks/kathryn_schulz_on_being_wrong.

4. J. Luft, *Group Processes: An Introduction to Group Dynamics*, 3rd ed. (New Yrok: McGraw-Hill Education, 1984), reprinted with permission.

5. M. Campbell and W. Fraser, *Team Charter*, 1995, used with permission.

6. C. N. Seashore and E. W. Seashore, *Check-Ins and Check-Outs*, 2006, permission granted from the Seashore family.

INDEX

V

W

ABOUT WENDY FRASER

Wendy Fraser has what the hip-hop genera-
tion calls "street cred." A veteran of more than
twenty-five years of experience in leadership
and team development, she excels at understanding human dynamics and organizational
development, and brings contagious energy
as a speaker and consultant. Wendy considers
herself a lifelong learner—she has a doctorate
and three master's degrees to back that up, but

she demonstrates it by creating the space where everyone can grow and
contribute. She truly believes that people have the wisdom and capacity
to learn and make things better, even in the worst of times. She has specifically studied trust and trust repair in groups for more than ten years
and actively consults with organizations on how to do it.

Wendy is an easy-to-talk-to person who really connects with people
of all ages and at any level in organizations. In addition to managing her
own consulting business, teaching at two universities, and serving her
community as an active volunteer, she has been honored as an international humanitarian for her work with developing leadership capacity in
youth around the world. Wendy loves spending time with her family: two
kids, two black labs, one husband, and one cat, who rules the house! In
her spare time, she is energized by creative projects like scrapbooking,
and she is *trying* to improve her photography skills.

www.WendyFraserConsulting.com

Printed in the United States
By Bookmasters